Withdrawn

In the Floating Army

GREGORY R. WOIROL

In the Floating Army

F. C. Mills on Itinerant Life in California, 1914

UNIVERSITY OF ILLINOIS PRESS
Urbana and Chicago

HV
4506
.C2
W65
1992

An earlier version of chapter 2 appeared as " 'Rustling' Oranges in Lindsay," *California History* 62 (Summer 1983): 82–97. Reprinted material appears herein by permission of the California Historical Society.

An earlier version of chapter 7 appeared as "Observing the IWW in California, May–July 1914," *Labor History* 25 (Summer 1984): 437–47. Reprinted material appears herein with the journal's permission.

© 1992 by the Board of Trustees of the University of Illinois
Manufactured in the United States of America
C 5 4 3 2 1

This book is printed on acid-free paper.

Library of Congress Cataloging-in-Publication Data

Woirol, Gregory R. (Gregory Ray), 1948–
    In the floating army : F. C. Mills on itinerant life in California, 1914 / Gregory
R. Woirol.
        p.   cm.
    Includes bibliographical references and index.
    ISBN 0-252-01800-1 (alk. paper)
    1. Tramps—California—History—20th century—Sources.   I. Title.
HV4506.C2W65   1992   305.5'68—dc20   90-21555

For Susan, Samantha, and Stephanie

Contents

Preface ix

Acknowledgments xi

Introduction 1

1. The Wheatland Riot, Kelley's Army, and F. C. Mills 5

2. "Rustling" Oranges in Lindsay 22

3. Work in a Sierra Lumber Camp 41

4. The Employment Agency Game 65

5. Walking the Roads 76

6. Riding the Rails 96

7. Observing the IWW 115

8. Conclusions 131

Notes 141

Bibliography 155

Index 163

Preface

Several years ago I received in the mail a large box of letters and personal papers of Columbia University economist Frederick C. Mills. I was interested in Mills's professional contributions in the 1920s and 1930s, and I had written to his elder son William to ask whether his father had left any records that might be of value in my research. Included in the box were several folders of materials that, at first glance, seemed to relate to itinerant labor. Since they were not relevant to the topic I was interested in at the time, I scanned them and set them aside. When I examined them again, much later, I soon became completely absorbed. I found a wide variety of papers that together provided a detailed account of a two-month journey Mills had taken disguised as a hobo in the summer of 1914.

I considered three possible approaches to using Mills's hobo papers: to write a general history of itinerant life in the United States in the pre–World War I period, using his papers as one of several sources; to write a local history, focusing more narrowly on the time period and area of his trip; or to produce an edited version of his papers. All three, I decided, had basic weaknesses. The first two would omit what is most valuable and interesting in Mills's writings—the liveliness of his firsthand account of a life "on the road." The third, while highlighting Mills's writing, would suffer because of the great amount of materials, their lack of structure, and repetition.

I therefore decided on a compromise: to produce a modified form of an edited version of his papers. I have organized his observations topically and have provided contextual material, but otherwise, as much as possible, I have let Mills tell his own story—often at length. This approach deals effectively with the drawbacks of simply presenting his papers, yet preserves the dozens of passages that could not be summarized or paraphrased without losing the vigor of Mills's writing.

Mills's original papers remain in the possession of his son William H. Mills. The records of his hobo trip include an 80-page "Record," which he typed from a daily journal he kept during his trip; five formal reports totaling about 75 pages, which he submitted to the California Commission of Immigration and Housing; nine short papers containing poems, outlines, and summaries, altogether about 55 pages, which he wrote after his journey; and the draft of a 163-page novel based on his experiences, which he began in the 1950s. Mills's other papers consist of dozens of letters to family members and colleagues, many newspaper clippings, and copies of several memorials written at his death. The quotations from Mills's writings used in this book come from these sources.

Acknowledgments

I have incurred many debts in writing this book. The foremost is to William H. Mills. His permission for me to use his father's papers and his willingness to help with requests for further information have made this study possible. Several colleagues read drafts of the manuscript and made helpful suggestions regarding organization, content, and style. I would like especially to thank Richard Archer, Myra Hart, Leslie Howard, Charles Laine, Donald Nuttall, and Stephen Overturf for their very useful comments on specific subjects or chapters. I am particularly grateful to Robert Marks for his comments and direction after reading the first complete draft of the manuscript. My greatest debt for friendly criticism is to Joseph Fairbanks, who read the entire manuscript three times and made copious suggestions; the book could not have been completed without his encouragement and support. I am also indebted to two anonymous readers for their thoughtful comments. These colleagues have saved me from many errors of omission and commission. I also wish to thank Richard Wentworth, my editor, for his interest and enthusiasm for the project, and Beth Bower for copyediting the manuscript with great care and insight. Finally, I would like to thank my wife Susan, who was always willing to take time away from her own work to visit libraries, read drafts, draw maps, or take photographs; her comments and advice are reflected in every page of this book.

Introduction

In Fresno on the twenty-first day of May, 1914, I slipped into
a pair of worn blue over-alls, an outworn coat, and a broken
down hat, slung a roll of blankets on my back, and started out
as a migratory laborer, of a type that is known variously as a
"hobo," "blanket stiff," "Bindle stiff," and "working stiff."

With these words, Frederick C. Mills began an account of the
two months he spent "on the road" in California in the summer of
1914.[1] Working as an investigator for the California Commission of
Immigration and Housing, he traveled the Central Valley of California between Fresno in the south and Redding in the north, taking
time out from his journey to "rustle" orange boxes in a packinghouse, to work as a "grader" for a company railroad in a Sierra lumber
camp, to investigate the activities of the Industrial Workers of the
World, and to talk with dozens of fellow hoboes. Mills kept a journal
as he traveled, recording his observations and his thoughts about
itinerant life in California. When he finished his trip and returned
to work with the Immigration Commission, he authored five reports
based on his findings. Years later he wrote a draft of a novel about
his trip. The firsthand account in these materials of a life that was
hidden from most U.S. citizens is a fascinating record of what he
once termed "the world of the submerged."[2]

The existence of an underclass of itinerant workers in the United
States had been recognized for fifty years before Mills began his trip.
Unemployed and migrant workers were commented on in the an-
tebellum period. Beginning in the 1870s, the number of men stealing
rides on the railroads, living in hobo "jungles," and wandering from
town to town started to rise rapidly. Around the turn of the century
several accounts of daily hobo life by curious investigators were published, including works by Walter Wyckoff, John J. McCook, Josiah

Flynt, and Jack London. It is rare to be able to add to these studies.
Mills's record, in its breadth and its insightful reflections, is an important contribution to these primary sources about itinerant life.[3]

Mills's writings chronicle the awakening of social consciousness
in a well-educated, intelligent urban progressive. When he began his
trip, Mills had no idea of what life was like for the masses of itinerant
and casual laborers who lived around him in California. It is evident
from his remarks that he started his journey with an adventurous
and lighthearted attitude, but the tone of his writing changed as he
was exposed to the daily experiences of itinerant workers. The life
that these men led distressed Mills, and he appealed forcefully in his
journal and reports for policies to ease their plight. Even so, he remained influenced by conventional attitudes about itinerant life. In
writing about "unemployables" on the road, for example, he tended
to categorize the men he met as the "worthy" and "unworthy" poor.
The inconsonance of being simultaneously sympathetic and judgmental was common among outsiders of the time who investigated
the underclass. As a result of this tension, Mills's writings are filled
with comments revealing his attempts to understand the complexities
of seasonal worker lifestyles, his reactions to the feelings of discontent
among the itinerant population, and his reflections on the juxtaposition of tragedy, humor, and adventure in daily life on the road.[4]

Mills's writings also show his struggle to conceptualize issues related to seasonal and casual work. The early discoverers of the "tramp
problem" in the 1870s often depicted itinerants as a dangerous class
that should be forcibly repressed. This attitude laid the foundation
for the enduring belief that migrant problems were due to individual
failings and character flaws. By 1914, the forces behind the existence
of the large class of floating workers were beginning to be better
understood. Robert Hunter, for example, in his classic 1904 study
of poverty, and W. Jett Lauck and Edgar Sydenstricker in a 1917
review of recent studies about labor conditions in the United States,
clearly put the blame for the existence of a large itinerant class on
the nature of the evolution of the U.S. economy since the Civil War.
Recent analyses of the pre–World War I era, including studies by
Herbert G. Gutman, Michael B. Katz, Alexander Keyssar, Kenneth
L. Kusmer, Eric H. Monkkonen, David Montgomery, and Daniel T.
Rodgers, among others, develop this theme in detail, explaining how
industrialization, unlimited immigration, and industrial employment

practices produced an environment of chronic irregular employment for the working class. Mills's writings were part of the body of work creating a growing awareness of the larger causes of itinerancy. His experience as a temporary member of the underclass led him to write his doctoral thesis on theories of unemployment, which contains one of the best reviews of the topic in his day. During his hobo journey he began to develop his ideas about these issues, which became central topics in his journal and reports, including the difficulties of understanding the causes of itinerant labor problems, of coming up with reasonable and adequate policy solutions, and of convincing others that these policies should be implemented.[5]

The main theme of Mills's observations also adds to our understanding of itinerant and seasonal laborers: as he put it at one point in his journal, there was "no way out for the most of them." A history of temporary work, Mills argued, severely limited opportunities for permanent employment. He found that the migrant cycle of hard physical labor followed by unemployment and a period on the road in search of a new job often led to ill health and dissipation. Constant pressures on itinerants led them to degenerate over time from strong, able workers to "derelicts in the prime of life." To Mills this tendency was "the most evil feature" of seasonal and casual labor.[6]

Ultimately, Mills's record is valuable because it is so well written. In telling the story of his trip through the Central Valley of California, he effectively and intelligently re-creates a whole world of early twentieth-century workers—the "world of the submerged." His record brings to life one of the major issues of his day while helping to rescue from obscurity the history of one of the most neglected classes in the development of the U.S. economy—casual, seasonal, and itinerant workers.

1

The Wheatland Riot,
Kelley's Army,
and F. C. Mills

I

On August 3, 1913, a riot erupted on the Durst hop ranch near Wheatland, California. Ralph Durst, part owner and manager of the ranch, had advertised in newspapers all over the state for 2,700 workers when, as he later admitted, he had only 1,500 jobs to fill. The 2,800 people who showed up in answer to the ads—half of whom were women and children—found themselves living in abominable conditions. The workers were given a barren field in which to set up camp where the temperature hovered near 105 degrees by midday. With only nine outdoor toilets, by the second day of the week before the riot the stench was overwhelming to the point that many cases of vomiting were reported. Durst had made no effective provision for garbage collection, and the camp was strewn with piles of rotting food scraps and refuse. The water supply also was inadequate; the wells were a mile from where the workers were picking, and two of them often pumped dry each day before sunup. Durst did not allow water to be trucked in, partly because his cousin, Jim Durst, had a concession to sell lemonade at a nickel a glass to the workers, who made from an average of $.78 to $1.90 per person per day. Local stores were forbidden to ship in supplies, and workers without transportation had to buy from a store on the ranch from which Durst received 50 percent of the profits.[1]

With these appalling conditions, unrest quickly mounted at the camp. The workers protested, and Industrial Workers of the World

(IWW) activists called a rally for Sunday, August 3. The workers
main grievance at the meeting was over living conditions, with the
rally leader Richard "Blackie" Ford at one point taking a sick infant
from its mother's arms and crying out, "It's for the kids we are doing
this!" The demonstration progressed peacefully until near its end.
As the meeting was ending and the workers were singing the famous
IWW song "Mr. Block," the local sheriff, a posse, and the district
attorney arrived. When the sheriff advanced to arrest the rally leaders,
a deputy fired a shot in the air—as he later said, "to sober the
crowd"—and fighting broke out. In the riot that followed four people
died, including the district attorney, a deputy sheriff, and two workers.
Many others were injured. Officials raised an immediate cry of alarm,
and within hours Governor Hiram Johnson sent four companies of
the National Guard to keep order around Wheatland. Police arrested
about one hundred workers immediately. During the following weeks,
IWW members were arrested all over the state in a panic that violated
the civil rights of dozens. The two IWW leaders at the camp rally,
Ford and Herman D. Suhr, were hunted down and eventually sen-
tenced to life imprisonment.

The Wheatland riot shocked the citizens of California. Seasonal,
itinerant, and migrant labor had been a significant factor in the California economy for forty years prior to the riot, but the seasonal
labor "problem" had not often entered the general public consciousness. Taking seasonal agricultural workers as an example, it is easy
to see why the public was—and still is—able to ignore migrant problems. The farm economy needs a cheap and ample supply of workers
for short intervals at particular times of the year. Farm employers
have no other use for this labor, and in the off-season their wish is
only for it to disappear. Since there is no work, this is what migrants
must do. Historically, the labor requirements of California agriculture
have been met (at different times and in different places) by American
Indian, Chinese, Japanese, Indian, Armenian, Filipino, and Mexican
workers. What these diverse groups have shared is their economic
role as a source of plentiful, temporary, and cheap labor.

The past one-hundred-year history of California's seasonal laborers
is one of powerless workers who have received only brief and scattered
moments of sympathetic attention from reform groups or government agencies. No writer on California labor history has found positive things to say about the status and treatment of California's

An overview of the hop pickers' camp on the Durst ranch taken the day before the Wheatland riot of August 3, 1913. The Archives of Labor and Urban Affairs, Wayne State University.

Hop pickers on the Durst ranch the day before the Wheatland riot. The Archives of Labor and Urban Affairs, Wayne State

migrants. The term "exploited" is an apt one to describe the experiences of many of these workers. If practices such as those used by Durst had been uncommon, the story of migrant and seasonal laborers would be different, but these conditions were not unusual—certainly not in Mills's time. It is not known with certainty how many people had to live with such conditions in California in the years before World War I. At the time of the Wheatland incident, the working and living conditions of migrants were almost unknown. The Wheatland riot created a reason to find out what they were.[2]

The march of Kelley's Army in the winter following the Wheatland riot provided another reason to investigate. One of the unknowns about seasonal migrant life was what itinerants did when work was no longer available. A partial answer to this question became evident in the fall of 1913 as thousands of seasonal employees migrated to the cities, creating an estimated 75,000 unemployed in San Francisco and Los Angeles. Unrest was at a particularly high level along the breadlines in San Francisco, and it soon became known that a "General Kelley" was organizing the unemployed and destitute of the city. In the late winter of 1913–14, Kelley had an "army" organized and ready to march to Washington, D.C. When the army gathered, officials in San Francisco quickly arranged ferry service to Oakland—where city officials just as quickly arranged police-escorted transportation to Sacramento. Outside of Sacramento the 1,500 men in the unemployment army were stopped and forced to make camp. With the governor of Nevada saying they would be driven back by force if they entered his state, and the sheriff of Contra Costa County threatening to "shoot them down in rows" if they turned back toward San Francisco, the army had nowhere to go. For a few days the city of Sacramento fed the motley band, but city officials soon became concerned by the expense and ordered the men to move on. When they refused to go, a rival army of eight hundred special deputy sheriffs appeared. Armed with pick handles and hoses supplied by the fire department, the deputies drove the army of the unemployed across the Sacramento River and into Yuba County, destroying their camp and provisions along the way. For two weeks Kelley's pathetic army camped across the river, with the eight hundred armed deputies guarding the city against their return. Three weeks later the army had dispersed, leaving only a remnant of the hardiest participants behind.[3]

The Wheatland riot and the march of Kelley's Army convinced public officials that there was a seasonal worker problem that required investigation. The level of interest was so high that an observer of events at the time was later led to comment that "there began such a widespread and agitated discussion of the condition of the state's casual workers, that the two years of 1913 and 1914 will be known in western labor history as the 'period of the migratory worker.' "[4]

The Californians' interest in labor issues was not an isolated local concern, but part of a nationwide awakening of interest in labor conflicts. The sense that labor-management relations were getting out of control was so pervasive that a federal Commission on Industrial Relations was created in June 1913 to study the issue. The commission spent two years traveling the country, holding hearings, and directing a research staff in a study of labor conditions in the United States covering the period 1910–15. Its final report came to eleven stout volumes and chronicled a period of labor and business violence unmatched in U.S. history.

Observers of the time discussed the likelihood of open class warfare—not as a theoretical possibility at some future date, but as a real possibility evolving out of current events. Although the level of conflict reached in industrial relations in the years before World War I was to diminish over the decades ahead, this hindsight was not available to those living through the era of open labor warfare. As Graham Adams, Jr., has noted in a history of the Industrial Relations Commission, the industrial violence of the time was a challenge to the very viability of a free society. It was one of the most important issues of the day, and the search for its causes and solution involved many of the leading progressives and reformers of the time.[5]

California was very much a part of the age of industrial violence, and its resident reformers were as affected by local conflicts as others were by events in their parts of the country. As a result of this new interest in labor problems, the Commission of Immigration and Housing was directed to turn its attention to the issue. When Governor Hiram Johnson had initially proposed the formation of such a commission in August 1912, he had intended that it devote its time to "investigate the immigration problems that will be presented to us with the opening of the Panama Canal, the distribution of the immigrants who will come to this state thereafter, and such other matters as may be necessary to prevent the congestion of population and the other evils that have arisen through lack of foresight and care in the eastern states." By the time of its formal organization in September 1913, the commission's mandate had been expanded to include all aspects of migrant and itinerant labor problems.[6]

The major impetus behind this change was the Wheatland riot in August. In its *First Annual Report* the commission announced its decision "to avail itself of this opportunity to conduct a careful investigation into the economic and social causes leading up to the riot." The commission's *Report on the Wheatland Hop-Fields Riot* was completed in March 1914 and officially issued with majority and minority views on June 1, 1914. The Wheatland report—one of the most vivid formal investigations written on seasonal labor in California—was authored by the commission's executive secretary, Carleton H. Parker.[7]

Before accepting this post, Parker had been a young economics professor at the University of California, Berkeley, with a personal and professional interest in current labor issues. His first assignment from the commission was to gather relevant background data and write the report on the Wheatland riot. Parker was appalled by the conditions he discovered. He concluded that the riot was an inevitable result of the way in which migrants were treated and forced to live. He also believed that their environment explained much about the contemporary strength of the revolutionary message of the IWW. In his view the problem was exacerbated by the public authorities' lack of understanding of the migrants' plight and their scant sympathy for it.[8]

In this environment of labor unrest and misunderstanding, which he believed had reached a critical stage, Parker searched for solutions. When he started as executive secretary, the Immigration Commission "lacked factual data . . . upon which to base a specific remedial program. It needed an over-all picture of California conditions for the purpose of allocating emphasis." As a result, thirty-five special reports were prepared, which became the foundation for the commission's programs of education, labor camp inspection, and urban housing inspection. The commission also undertook a survey of unemployment in the state (*Report on Unemployment*, December 1914) and lobbied for the creation of a series of state employment bureaus. After Parker left the commission in the fall of 1914, he used the information he had collected to write one of the first careful studies of the itinerant labor issue in California.[9]

Only three of the thirty-five background reports written under Parker in 1914 were published. The Wheatland riot report was one of these, and two others were included as sections of the 1914 *Report on Unemployment.* Brief descriptions of all the reports were appended to the *First Annual Report* of the commission in January 1915. A selection of titles from the appendix indicates the range of commission interests and the extent of its investigations: "The Floating Laborer in California," "Report on 'Kelley's Army,' " "The Berry Picking and Fruit Canning Industries of Sonoma County," "The Orange Industry of Central California," "An Economic Survey of a Sierra Lumber Camp," "The Employment Agency Situation in California," "The Wheatland Hop Field Riot," "Preliminary Report on the I.W.W. in California," "Southern European Farmers in the Bay Region," and "Tenement House Conditions in San Francisco." One of the staff members Parker hired to help him compile this firsthand information was Frederick Mills, one of his former students at Berkeley.[10]

II

Since Mills's work with the commission is the focus of this study, it is important to know something about him. Family clippings, letters, and copies of memorials reveal aspects of the personality of the young man who went out on the road as one of Parker's boys in 1914. Born in Santa Rosa, California, in 1892 and reared in Oakland, several incidents from his early years indicate that he liked risk and adventure.[11]

A January 1910 unfurling of the Senior Class banner from the roof of Oakland High School, for example, resulted in Mills and six other seniors being collared by the Oakland police and hauled off to the city jail in a police wagon. After an hour's detention and intervention by the superintendent of schools, Mills and his compatriots were released with a stern rebuke. The escapade got his picture in the local paper. In the summer of 1913, after his junior year in college, Mills signed on as a waiter on the U.S. army transport ship *Thomas* and spent the summer cruising from San Francisco to Hawaii and the Philippines and back. And the *San Francisco Bulletin*

F. C. Mills in 1913 in his junior-year class photo. From the yearbook of the University of California, Berkeley, *Blue and Gold,* 1914.

F. C. Mills (in the rickshaw on the left) in a family photo taken when he was in the Philippines in 1913 during his summer trip as a waiter on the U.S. army transport ship *Thomas.*

of July 3, 1916, reported that Frederick Mills, "a young Berkeley college professor" (he was a part-time assistant while completing his M.A.), had won fifty dollars in a *Bulletin* treasure hunt. The hunt had involved a mass of people, a fast ferry to Oakland from San Francisco, a twenty-minute search of a room at the Hotel Oakland, and a final speed-limit-breaking race to a second location, where the "pot of gold" was concealed. His picture appeared in the paper again, this time as a dapper young man wearing a derby.

Shortly after Mills completed his Ph.D. in 1917 he enlisted in the armed services. Transferred later in the year to France for training, Mills was commissioned in 1918 as a second lieutenant in the field artillery. He served with the 150th Field Artillery and the 316th Field Artillery and saw temporary duty with the English Eleventh Division Artillery. Promoted to first lieutenant in 1918, he completed his military service in April 1919.

The most influential adventure of Mills's youth with respect to his later professional life came after he left Berkeley as a Phi Beta Kappa graduate with a B.A. degree in economics. Hired by Carleton H. Parker as a special agent for the California Commission of Immigration and Housing in May 1914, Mills's first assignment was the two-month trip he took as a hobo in 1914. During his weeks on the road, he took the name of Fred Carr, joined the IWW, lived in jungles, and slept in haystacks. The experience had a lasting impact on him, and he returned to his notes and reports several times in later life. His M.A. and Ph.D. theses, both on contemporary theories of unemployment, were motivated by the problems he encountered as an agent for the Immigration Commission.[12]

Mills enjoyed a highly successful life, both personally and professionally. Married in 1919, he had a strong sense of family, which led him to maintain close contacts and a regular correspondence with his parents and, later, his children. His letters reveal that he had a lifelong love of poetry, which he apparently acquired from his mother. In 1932 he had printed, at his own expense, one hundred copies of a collection of her poems. He also wrote verse himself, entertaining fellow hoboes during his tramping days and professional colleagues in later life. His poem "Of Friday and Edie and Ayres" was a hit at the 1937 American Statistical Association meetings, and was published in the conference proceedings.[13]

Mills generally was conservative, but in the 1930s he voiced agreement in principle with the goals of the Roosevelt administration (although he had doubts about the long run because he felt "that no man is able to regulate the complex economy we have today, in spite of all the assurance which may appear in spoken or written words"), and in the late 1940s he was among those advocating nuclear disarmament. At times a fierce defender of his opinions, Mills consequently was called "Turk" by his friends. A late 1920s exchange of letters with Simon Kuznets, for example, over a criticism Kuznets made about one of Mills's articles, led to a demand from Mills to "support [your] statement with specific and detailed references, or to withdraw it." Kuznets withdrew it and apologized. Mills also became involved in a long-running dispute with a New England power company over changes in the level of a lake, which he alleged would ruin his summer home. His convictions also led him to support colleagues who asked for his help. He worked with the U.S. State Department and the American Friends Service Committee to help a Spanish translator of one of his books who had been imprisoned by the Franco regime, and he stoutly defended a former student who was tried for disloyalty during the late 1940s.[14]

Mills, however, did not actively seek conflict. A major contributor in a 1920s debate over methodology in economics, he avoided arguments and was willing to accept other points of view. His approach in his professional work was perhaps best indicated in a late 1950s exchange of letters with his son Robert, where Mills recalled "tender memories of [John Dewey's] class in 1916–17" and claimed that "I have always been sympathetic to pragmatism." To Mills, pragmatism meant acceptance of the fact that we live in a world "in which knowledge is necessarily incomplete (but expanding), in which ends and means are intertwined, and in which ends as well as means are subject to change." But, Mills held, "this is not to say that acceptance should be passive. Man is a struggling, growing, *reaching* animal. In dealing with the problems that constantly confront him he grows in understanding." This position was consistent with his claim thirty years earlier that economic knowledge was "statistical" in nature, meaning that economic relations could not be known with certainty and completeness.[15]

Mills also had a rich sense of humor and enjoyed making small bets on political or economic events. His losses included dollar bills sent through the mail to John Maynard Keynes, Claire Booth Luce, and often old California friends Allan Sproul, president of the Federal Reserve Bank of New York, and Robert Gordon Sproul, president of the University of California. His close personal attachments extended beyond his family circle, with many friendships lasting over decades, and they included not only New York colleagues but others across the country.

Mills's professional career was all that one could hope for in terms of recognition and success. Both Berkeley and Columbia offered him positions when he returned from service in World War I and a short period of study at the London School of Economics. The Economics Department at Berkeley "was very desirous" of having Mills, but he decided to stay in New York, later writing that he was a "renegade Native Son of the Golden West, actually preferring New York and Vermont to the glories of California." An early member of the National Bureau of Economic Research, he published numerous works, including four books and, for the bureau, several bulletins and occasional papers. His first book, *Statistical Methods*, went through three editions. He enjoyed collecting stories about the odd places people encountered his statistics book, including Ankara, Turkey, a village in central China, a pirated edition in Russia, and, his favorite, "bored British officers in a German prison camp [who] found a single copy, which became the basis of a self-taught course in statistics for a group of them." In 1940 the Social Science Research Council selected his book *The Behavior of Prices* as one of the best social science contributions of the 1920s. In 1934 he was elected president of the American Statistical Association, and in 1940 he was president of the American Economic Association. A long history of public service included acting as an adviser to the chief of Army Ordnance during World War II, leading a project to appraise the cost of living index, and directing an evaluation of the operation of all federal statistical agencies. An original associate editor of *Econometrica* and a charter member of the Econometric Society, he received honorary degrees from Berkeley in 1947 and from Columbia in 1961.[16]

The overall picture of Mills is one of an agreeable man to know who was satisfied with his personal and professional life. After he accepted a position at Columbia, there is little suggestion of great drama or tragedy in his life, but rather an impression of good order and good times. His most active years professionally were from the early 1920s through the early 1950s. During this period his publications were regular and numerous. He had a heart attack in early 1953 that forced him to slow down. He resigned from the National Bureau of Economic Research in that year and retired from Columbia University in 1959. Mills died in 1964.

III

Mills began his hobo journey in late May 1914 as a normal railroad passenger, "riding the cushions," south through the Central Valley of California (Map 1). The Central Valley is actually comprised of two river valleys—the Sacramento Valley north of the delta area around the city of Sacramento and the San Joaquin Valley south of the delta (Map 2). It is a huge, extraordinarily fertile agricultural area that runs parallel to the Pacific coastline. Bordering the valley on the west are coastal ranges of low mountains, and to the east the valley meets the Sierra Nevadas. Sixty years before Mills took his journey this vast area was primarily a wasteland of deserts and marshes. After the gold rush era the potential of the valley began to be realized as it began to fill with farms and people. By Mills's day the transformation of the valley to a major agricultural region was well on its way to completion. The great canals and dams that water the landscape today were years away, but rivers and wells provided adequate water at the time and supported the system of intensive agriculture that has characterized the area ever since.

Another feature of life in the Central Valley was also well developed by the time Mills took his trip: agriculture was on a large-scale commercial basis, with few small-scale family farms. This pattern first appeared in California during the wheat-farming years of the 1870s. The expectation at the time was that the gigantic wheat ranches would be divided up over time and replaced by family-sized farms, as had been the case in the Midwest, but when the transition from wheat to orchard and vegetable crops came in the 1880s and 1890s, this did not happen. California farms remained on a massive scale, in large part because of the availability of large numbers of seasonal workers. By the time Mills took his hobo journey, the existence of large-scale commercial agriculture was accepted by California farmers as both natural and right.[17]

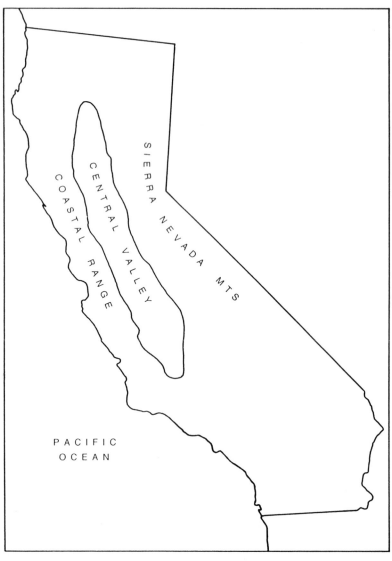

Map 1. Central Valley of California

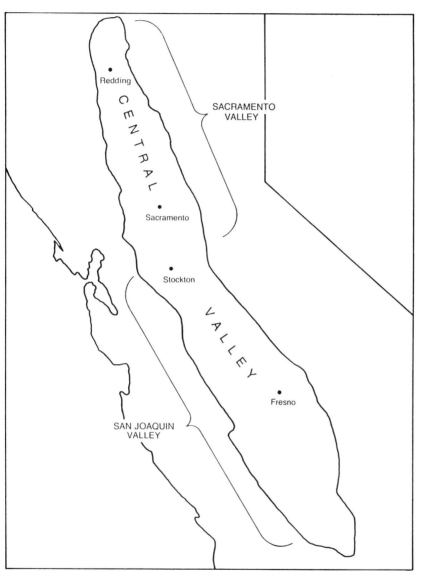

Map 2. Sacramento Valley and San Joaquin Valley

Mills's journey into the Central Valley had two major segments (Map 2). Starting from San Francisco, he first took a one-month trip south to the middle of the San Joaquin Valley, then turned north and spent the next month traveling in the Sacramento Valley. Focusing on working conditions in seasonal industries during his trip to the south, he wrote reports on the orange industry, on the lumber industry, and on road construction. He did not seek work during his time in the Sacramento Valley and instead spent his month in the north crossing and recrossing the same area between Redding and Sacramento by foot, car, and train. Many of his most important observations about itinerant life and about the IWW came from this portion of his trip.

Mills completed his investigations in late July and returned to Immigration Commission headquarters in San Francisco. He did not go back out on the road again. Although his papers do not reveal why he concluded his trip at this time, Carleton H. Parker was busy preparing reports and testimony for hearings before the U.S. Commission on Industrial Relations in San Francisco, and it is likely that Mills's help was needed. Mills worked with the Immigration Commission for another year, leaving in August 1915 to begin graduate work at Berkeley. During the rest of his year with the commission, his work included surveys of urban housing conditions and a study of the practices of public and private employment agencies.[18]

IV

In a 1915 essay on casual labor, Parker described early twentieth-century California as "a state of summer employment." According to Parker, "of the 150,000 migratory workers employed in the summer, a mass of direct and indirect information indicates that fully 100,000 face sustained winter unemployment." He was not alone in this assessment of the California economy. In a contemporary survey of national labor conditions, W. Jett Lauck and Edgar Sydenstricker concluded that "probably no more striking example of extremely seasonal industries exists than in California" and claimed that "the seasonal irregularity of employment is so great that there has grown up a large class of migratory homeless laborers." John A. Fitch, in a summary of hearings by the U.S. Commission on Industrial Relations, agreed that "most of the labor in California is seasonal in character" and declared that "there is a migratory class of labor in California because there must be. Without them the industries on which California's fame depends could not exist."[19]

It is difficult to know how many workers were part of the itinerant labor force in California at the time. Accurate current employment data were not collected until decades later. Parker's description of the state's economy is supported, however, by the fact that seasonal forces even dominated manufacturing in California. The minimum monthly manufacturing employment in California in 1914 was 119,688 in January. The maximum was 161,072 in August. The percentage that the minimum formed of the maximum (74.3 percent) was the forty-third lowest of the forty-eight states, indicating a greater seasonality of manufacturing employment than normal.[20]

Mills agreed with the above evaluations by his contemporaries and wrote a lengthy description of the state's economy, which he intended as an introduction to a series of articles based on his hobo experiences. Claiming that "California is distinctively the home of the itinerant, worker and vagrant alike," Mills found that there were essentially three major groups among the floating class: workers turned out each winter by industries of the state, seasonal workers who came to winter in California from other states, and nonworkers, "the vagrants, cripples, 'bums,' defectives, [and] yeggs." His attempt to understand "something of the various phases of this migratory life, of the traveling and working conditions under which live some of those who help make up our armies of the unemployed," began with a visit to the orange-growing region around Lindsay in the San Joaquin Valley.[21]

2

"Rustling" Oranges
in Lindsay

Mills has begun today and he and Brissenden are making
remarkably fine progress in organizing their field for the immediate survey beginning next week.

I

Carleton H. Parker notified Simon Lubin, president of the Immigration and Housing Commission, of Mills's hiring in a letter dated
May 15, 1914.[1] Mills's first assignment was to go out on the road
in the role of an itinerant worker. "The main purpose of the work,"
according to a report Mills wrote after his trip, "was the observation
of the actual traveling and living conditions of the vast army of
California itinerants." Parker thought the place to begin these observations was the orange-growing areas of Tulare County near the
town of Lindsay because "press despatches a few days previously had
announced that there was an immediate demand for hundreds of
workers for the harvesting and packing of the Valencia orange crop
in the Tulare district." Since the announcements of job vacancies in
Lindsay were similar to those that had created the problems at Wheatland the year before, Parker wanted to know if the ads were accurate.[2]
Mills left for Lindsay one week after he was hired by the commission. His notes do not discuss his expectations, but it is evident
from their tone that he left the Bay Area with a determination to do
an excellent job. Telegrams and letters in Immigration Commission
records show that there was frequent contact between Mills and the
commission's San Francisco office during his stay in Lindsay. The
businesslike nature of these communications indicates that Mills ap-

proached his trip seriously. His enthusiasm for the job is suggested by a description he wrote of how he disguised himself as a hobo: "Since last Thursday, when I changed my clothes at Fresno, I have been about the raggedest-looking hobo you ever saw. With old clothes, a broken-down hat, hair cut close, and a roll of blankets on my back, I don't think you'd speak to me if you met me." He thought his disguise a good one, but his days on the road began comically as he kept running into people he knew. On the way by train from Fresno to Exeter:[3]

> Imagine how I felt when a fair damsel, at some little station on the way, looked me over about five times, then walked up to me with hand extended, and said, "Why, Mr. ———, where are you going?" There wasn't even a squirrel hole near by, so I had to brazen it out. I murmured something about a "trip," but I could hardly explain myself. The following day I tramped into Lindsay from Exeter, and about the first person I met was a boy from Berkeley named Mouser. I was afraid to tell anything of my real business, so I could not explain my appearance to him. I think I'll have to paint myself black to prevent being recognized.[4]

One of a string of small towns along the western foothills of the Sierra Nevadas, Lindsay was surrounded by orange groves. The area had not been a citrus-growing region for long, however. The first major crop in Tulare County, from the 1870s to the 1890s, had been wheat. Between 1890 and 1910, the wheat ranches gave way to orchards and vineyards. Still later, cotton and olives became major crops.[5]

When Mills arrived at Lindsay, the yearly orange harvest was nearing its peak. As he had feared, the ads that had drawn him to the area were misleading. He reported to the commission:

> In place of the expected dearth of men described by the despatches which had gone out over all the state I found idle men on every street corner, and groups of a dozen or more along the tracks near the station. Except for one packing house which had a sign up stating that packers were wanted (skilled workers) there was absolutely no sign of a shortage of help. . . . The only possible explanation for the story that 500 more men were

needed is that certain of the growers and packers were desirous
of having on hand during the week or so of highest prices a
supply of men ample for the picking and packing. If several
hundred extra came in incidentally, why, the town police would
have a trifle more work. In this case the expected rush due to
the possibility of getting especially high prices did not material-
ize, and men had been brought to town to lie idle around the
tracks.[6]

This system of advertising to attract workers to seasonal jobs was
made famous in the 1930s by John Steinbeck in *The Grapes of Wrath*
when he had the Joad family lured to California by the promise of
nonexistent jobs after they lost their dust-bowl farm. Investigations
by agents of the U.S. Commission on Industrial Relations revealed
that this method of hiring migrant workers in Mills's time was common throughout the United States. In a December 1914 report on
"Labor Market Conditions in the Harvest Fields of the Middle West,"
for example, William Duffus cited many instances of the use of ex-
aggerated advertising. He quoted the county clerk of Rooks County,
Kansas, as saying, "We always estimate far more than are needed as
we are on the end of the railroad and men stop off before they get
here." Duffus wrote at length on the evils created by this practice in
terms of lower wages and unemployment, adding the comment that
"the Commission should walk up and down the streets of little cities
like Oakley and Colby, Kansas; Huron and Redfield, South Dakota;
and Casselton, North Dakota, and watch the men who sit along the
curbs in long rows, crowd the side walks, lean against buildings, and
hang around the railroad stations waiting—always waiting—for some
farmer to come into town to hire a hand; and note the hungry, tired
and despondent and sometimes sullen looks on the faces of these
men."[7]

Within California these hiring practices yielded identical results.
According to Carleton H. Parker's report on the Wheatland riot, the
clash was due in large part to conditions created by misleading advertising, which had attracted far more workers to the Durst hop
ranch than could be hired. Mills found the same situation when he
arrived in Lindsay, but he was lucky. Soon after he arrived, "I was
addressed by a young fellow who had just given up his job of 'rustler'
with the Drake Citrus Association, and was told that I might be able

to get on there. Fortunately the vacancy was still open, and I was hired at 25 cents an hour."[8]

Mills began work in the Drake packinghouse on May 22. For the next several days he experienced firsthand the life of a casual laborer. He did the work they did, ate the meals they ate, and slept in the places they slept. He learned quickly how to survive in these circumstances, and he began to learn about the effects of this life on those who had to live it everyday.

II

Early in his journal, Mills provided an overview of working conditions in the Drake packinghouse. Because of the space needed for storing the fruit, the packinghouse was spacious and well ventilated. With a crew of about fifty, sanitation facilities were satisfactory. Work lasted from ten to twelve hours a day during the peak months of May (for Valencia oranges) and November (for Navels), for six or seven days a week. Drake's packed between 1,500 and 1,600 boxes of oranges a day, paying its packers $4 1/2$ cents a box. The women packers took from nine to twenty-one minutes to pack a box, depending on the size of the oranges and the skill of the worker, for a daily wage ranging from about $1.15 to a maximum of $4.50 for a ten-hour day. The packing process in general was described briefly in Mills's journal:[9]

Sunday, May 24

The process of grading and packing oranges is simple but interesting. The boxes are brought in directly from the field and trucked to the "dumper." Here they are dumped on a moving spillway, and lifted by a simple contrivance to another moving spillway which carries them past four "separators." These separate the fruit into two grades, leaving one grade on the spillway and throwing the other on a second spillway. The spillways then carry the fruit into two graders, at each of which about a dozen packers work. The graders separate the fruit mechanically according to its size. A certain number of oranges of each size go into a box, the number varying from 324 for the smallest to 96 for the large oranges. Each size must be packed differently into the box, there being some ten different packing systems.

Mills was interested in providing more than a description of the work done in the industry, however. The main purpose of his journey was to learn about the people who worked in seasonal industries. As a result, he spent much time in his journal writing about the people he met. At several points, he described the workers inside Drake's:

May 22, 1914

There are about 24 packers, women and girls. About one-half of them are local people, farmers wives and daughters, country type. Rest come up from the South for the orange crop. Type prevailingly American. A few dark southern Europeans, but of the Americanized type; all literate.

Men American type; some local, some travel with crop. When owners here want this type they send south for them. Moral tone apparently healthy.

Most of the packers were girls or young women, although Mills saw a few older married women. Workers who did not already live in the local area boarded at various hotels and lodging houses at rates of six to eight dollars a week. He found conditions at these hotels satisfactory. His main impression of the people he met at Drake's was that they were "independent; most of them skilled in their lines, so [they] cannot be imposed on. They are the better class of migratory worker. Most of them pleasant and affable."[10]

Although the working conditions in the packinghouse appeared reasonable to Mills, the longer he worked at Drake's, the more he understood the difficulty of adjusting to a life of intermittent unskilled work:

Sunday, May 24

Have half a day of no work so can catch up with my records. What a relief to sit down and write.

Friday night I was about as tired as one could be. For several months I had done no physical work to speak of and worked my mind over time, what with closing exes [examinations], etc.

Friday I had arisen at 5:15 after sleeping some six hours by the road. Walked 7½ miles along a R.R. track before breakfast. Started work as a "rustler" at 8:30. "Rustling" is admittedly the hardest job in a packing house. This place—Drakes—has been unable to keep any "rustler" more than 3–4 days. There are 2

The McLee Brothers Orchard, West Lindsay, California, 1905. Harold G. Schutt Collection, Department of Special Collections, Henry Madden Library, California State University, Fresno.

Inside the Randolph Fruit Company orange packinghouse in Lindsay, California, showing supervisors, packers, and rustlers. Harold G. Schutt Collection, Department of Special Collections, Henry Madden Library, California State University, Fresno.

rustlers here, each attending to about a dozen packers; when a
packer wishes a box, she yells sharply, "box." The rustler
punches her card and carries the box to a bench from ten to
twenty yards away, where a top is put on it.

Each box weighs 70 lbs. From 500 to 700 are carried in a day.
I worked at this till 9 P.M. Friday night with two hours off for
meals. By the time I finished my feet were blistered, my hands
were torn, my arms almost numb, my back aching, and each of
my thighs with a red hot sear across it where the edges of the
box rubbed. I no longer wonder why there are so many I.W.W.s.
Why are there not more anarchists?

Although Mills's first reference to the union the Industrial Workers
of the World and the hardship of "rustling" was facetious in tone,
as he continued to work at Drake's his views became more sympathetic with the workers he was observing. At one point, he commented on the effect of the long working day on himself and, at
another, on women workers in the packinghouse:[11]

May 25—6:30 P.M.

Yesterday—Tuesday—the other rustler quit—claiming that the
work was too hard. After using several of his regular force,
[Drake] put on the job a hardy-looking youth who had been
handling lumber all winter.

I was put on the grader on which all the southern packers
work, and they kept me on the jump all day. They work just
about twice as fast as the local packers on the other grader. I
was carrying boxes steadily all day long, being deprived of the
brief resting periods I had had on the other job. Constantly,
unremittingly, the cry of "box," enunciated shrilly, harshly, irri-
tably, mandatorily, pleadingly, angrily, nasally, and in various
combinations of these tones, would ring out in twenty different
sharps and flats. Every time I thought I had a moment to rest,
to relax the tortured tendons and muscles in my arms and back
the shrill cry "box" would come from three or four different
sections. How I cursed that sound before the day closed. "The
damned," me thought, "use that word in Hell." Or more probably it is the little devils who do the damning who use it.

Sunday, May 24

Lunch revives one wonderfully, and we come back at one o'clock ready for another spell of work. I am beginning to get hardened to the job now and am learning something of the art of handling a box with the least amount of effort. The women stand the work and the long hours well except some of the girls who visibly pale and wilt as the long afternoon drags on. Tho their work is not heavy they are compelled to stand on their feet for from ten to twelve hours a day, and it cannot but do them harm.

Does the organization of modern industry demand the development of a class of female workers who are worn out, ready for the scrap heap at thirty?

Mills did not answer his question, but the fact that he raised it is an indication that he was impressed by the difficulty of the life he saw. Besides describing the work inside the packinghouse, Mills recounted snatches of conversations and significant incidents, which are among the most vivid parts of his journal. They give us a feeling for the character and the humor of the people who worked in Drake's:

Sunday, May 24

The conversation among the packers is often interesting—tho usually made up only of female gossip of the packing house. One says to another, "Do you belong to a church?" "No, don't you like it," is the answer. "I just wondered," says the first. "Well, one doesn't have to be a Christian to belong to a church," says the second, to justify herself. How much truth was in that inverted remark.

Or perhaps a box is to be sent back to be repacked—"Here," says the boss, "Take this back to ——— and if she doesn't like it tell her to go to Hell." The American boss is above all things a gentleman.

May 25—6:30 P.M.

Several of the men working in the place are exceptionally interesting as types. One in particular—a man of about 45—who grades fruit and does other odd jobs, getting probably not over 25 cents or 30 cents an hour attracted my attention. Over six feet tall, with a splendid frame, he has a face marked by strong and forceful lines. A good forehead, a strong chin, "an eye like Mars, to threaten and command," with an iron grey mustache and dark grey hair, one would pick him out as a leader of men. I searched in vain for a trace of weakness to explain his present position. I could only find something approaching it in the almost servile way, like a dog fawning his master, in which he addressed the boss. It was the tone in which he said "Harry" to him, with a peculiar little servile twist, that gave the lie to all the promise of his form and features.

There was another man, a grader, with drawling speech, and dark drooping mustache who somehow made me think of Bret Harte and Mark Twain, and of faro and poker and all that goes with early California. A dry quizzical humor fitted well his drawling speech. Once when the grader was blocked and had to be stopped immediately I shouted to him to shut off the flow of oranges. He did so and then he drawled out slowly, "By God, a man has to have on a uniform around here to give orders like that." The laugh that followed was at my expense.

May 24—7 P.M.

The only thing that broke the monotony of the afternoon's work today was a man's quitting his job. Some "culls" as they are called, that should have been thrown out by the separators were passed thru-. Drake saw them and yelled at one of the separators, "What the Hell's the matter with you? Don't you know a cull when you see it?" The fellow said nothing for a moment, then picked up an orange and threw it violently down again. "Well, I guess I quit here." "And a damn good thing," said the boss, "You don't know a thing about grading."

It seems to be a characteristic of the American type worker to take no "lip" from the boss. He is seldom so tied to a job but that he will throw it up if the boss curses him. The derelict gardener at Fresno, with bleary, beer-soaked eyes, said he would take sass from nobody. My fellow-rustler here advises talking right back to the boss and taking no "guff" from him. The job is not dear to the heart of the transient worker. This independent attitude does not hold true of the Oriental, and to a less extent than among workers of the American type does it hold true of representatives of the "New Immigration."

III

Working inside Drake's was not the entire life of the people Mills was observing. He did not write about the life of married workers outside of Drake's, but his own experience as an itinerant provided a graphic illustration of the daily existence of many seasonal workers. Mills's account of his first night in Lindsay contains a particularly striking description of dinner in a workingman's lodging house:

Sunday, May 24
"Dad" is quite a unique specimen of the old type innkeeper. The place he flatters (or graces) with the title of "hotel" is a ramshackle, dilapidated old building of two stories. The proprietor's bed room is the sitting room and parlor but is only used as such when the front porch can not be used. The men gather on this porch and exchange pleasant amenities, couched usually in the most vilifying and uncomplimentary terms, with the passers-by. Meals here are most interesting. When one enters the dining room he is likely to think he has gone into a fly culture station. Flies of all shapes and sizes buzzing in close harmony in a magnificent chorus containing bassos, tenors, altos, sopranos and many others not usually listed. Screens are kept on the windows to keep the flies in.
The food is placed on the table in great dishes from which one helps himself. Meanwhile mine host—small, rather corpulent, red-faced, getting a little old and testy—stands by the table and directs operations, keeping up a flow of conversation. When a guest asks for something mine host bellows forth in a stentorian and strident tone, "Potatoes, mam," "Butter, mam." The "mam" who attends to these wants is a meek thin little woman, evidently the wife of the host, who hurries back and forth, here and there, trying to supply all that is wanted. If she is a little slow, or too busy to come immediately, mine host picks up the plate, repeats his hoarse call, and thrusts it into her hand. She bears a long-suffering face but says nothing. If there come a time when the meek shall inherit the earth, a large share of it shall surely accrue to the wife of "Dad," proprietor of Dad's Hotel, in Lindsay, Tulare County, California.

After dinner at Dad's, Mills had to find a place to spend the night. In an account he wrote after his trip, he captured the kinds of experiences that were daily fare for many itinerant workers:

> I was given a bitter example that night of some of the difficulties the migratory worker has to cope with if he is desirous of remaining in the ranks of respectable citizens. Tired and worn out after the day's work I was anxious to get a bed in one of the lodging houses in Lindsay. With my bundle on my back I walked up to the Hinman House, at which, I knew, some of the orange workers boarded. Doubtful eyes looked me over, and I was refused a room, or a bed. On trying again, at a similar place, I was again refused. I applied finally to "Dad," with whom I had had supper. "Dad" refused me a single room, and a bed with sheets, but showed me a bunk without sheets, in a squalid little room already holding one sleeper. A look at the dirty clothes of the bunk convinced me that there were original occupants whose claims to possession were prior to mine.[12]

Unwilling to sleep with the fleas and bedbugs, Mills had to search again for a place to sleep. His journal carries his story through the next morning when he had to return to work:

Sunday, May 24

So I left Dad's place, not without some misgivings for it was now half-past nine and I was dog-tired and weary. At the first corner I was accosted by Macyntire, yclept briefly "Mac," a boarder at Dad's—an apparently rather shiftless local character, strong, hearty, eating a ploughman's meal, but as long as I was there going to work "tomorrow." (O mystic word of the southland, many and faithful be the devotees who worship at thy shrine.) "Mac" referred me to the livery stable, offering the right to use the magic of his name, which presumably was an open sesame to whatever of good Lindsay boasted. The night was soft and delicate, however, glowing with a myriad mystic twinklings, and I chose to "flop" beneath the stars.

The country around Lindsay is devoted almost exclusively to the orange crop, so there were no hospitable hay cocks inviting me. I spread my blankets in some tall grass by the side of the road, took off my shoes and socks only, and rolled in. As I was dozing off I heard some passing men refer to the "damn hobo" by the roadside, but it disturbed me not. The ground was hard, but to my weary bones and aching muscles a stone bed would have seemed like a downy feather mattress.

The next morning, Saturday, I woke with the sun staring me in the face. Antaeus-like, the contact with old earth had filled me with new life, and even the prospect of "rustling" 600 orange boxes was not altogether unpleasant to me. Performing my ablutions at a wayside hydrant I breakfasted sumptuously on "bacon and" at George's Place, a flaming sign above which announced that the best twenty-five-cent meal in town could be secured within. The place was filled with working men in their shirtsleeves, men working in the picking and packing of oranges. The summer season lasts here less than thirty days, during which time Lindsay is a veritable hive of industry. . . .

At George's and elsewhere I could not help observing how these men swallow their food. Ten minutes at most is sufficient time for a large meal to be stowed away, root and branch. Little is said while eating, attention being confined strictly to the business on hand.

Saturday, Mills's second day at Drake's, was another full day of work. Afterward he again had to find a place to sleep. His second night as a hobo was even more difficult and discouraging than his first. In an extended journal section he described his experience outside of Drake's from Saturday night through Sunday morning:

Sunday, May 24

Before we close I ask Drake for some money due me, as my cash assets amount to about a dollar. Instead of money I am given a meal ticket—"Good for five dollars in meals" at George's Place. I am told to come to work at one o'clock the next day—Sunday.

I am determined that for at least one night I will have a good sleep. So after supper I set out with my blankets on my back to find a hay-stack. But my fond hopes are doomed to be blasted. With blistered feet and aching bones I tramp for a mile and a half out of Lindsay. On the right of me there are oranges, on the left of me oranges, behind me and in front of me oranges. But nowhere is there hay to be seen. As well might I be seeking the proverbial needle as the haystack itself. I curse volubly mentally and swear that I will find a haystack. It is haying season all along the valley and I know there are bound to be stacks somewhere. But the God of Ironical Disappointments has been withholding his cruelest barb. The sky has been dark all afternoon, but I have feared no rain at this season. But now I feel a drop on my head—I turn my face up to investigate and feel more drops. It rains. With black thoughts, breathing direful imprecations I turn to retrace the weariest mile and a half on God's earth. I don't know why I turn back as I don't know where to go when I get there. They have refused me a room at two hotels. "Dad's" dirty little bunk is probably still empty of all save its socialistic community of original occupants. How I long for the flesh pots again. Stern, hard and real has life become. I, a petted product of a pampered civilization, feel the stern pressure of reality. Night is coming on in a strange country, and I am refused a place to lay my "weary bones." "Yea, I wept when I remembered Zion." My dark musings were made darker as, in following what appeared to be a path across a field, I was peremptorily ordered by a harsh voice to "Get out of that orchard." I did so.

Footsore, weary and disheartened I reached Lindsay—a proletaire in search of a place to lay his head. Remembering "Mac's" advice I tried the livery stable. Even the magic of that wonderful name failed to touch the heartstrings of the owner. I was refused. I headed then for the railroad track, that lodestone that draws all such "blanket-stiffs" as I. There are a long string of empty box cars but all of them appear to be locked. The rain is now getting quite heavy and I begin to fear that I am in for a wet and uncomfortable night. But the goddess who watches over homeless vagrants smiled then. I find in the long string a car with an unlocked door. Old it is and dirty, the sides and the floor dust-covered. But the sound of the rain on the roof is good to hear.

Sleeping in a side-door Pullman in a region infested with tramps of varying degrees of viciousness is not an altogether alluring prospect. It is easy to conjure up all sorts of dangers, and bloody tales flock to one's mind. But I decide that these fears are but painted devils after all. Besides, am I not now myself a blood brother of the road?

At about twelve o'clock I was awakened by the striking of a match in the car. Two homeless wanderers like myself were looking in out of the rain for a lodging place for the night. I gave them greeting and they crawled in. They were evidently of the so-called hobo class "blowed in the glass" I judged from their conversation and their language. One had a blanket while the other had none. As the latter, whom the other called "Smoke," prepared to "flop," rolled up in some old clothes he had, he remarked philosophically, but with depths of bitterness in his tone, "This is a damn hard world—a damn hard world." For such as you, Smoke, it is a damn hard world. Not for you is it to know the pleasures of tender nursing, of careful upbringing, the joys of a home, of a respected position in the community, the satisfaction of a life work well done. You and your kind are sworn brothers to grim Necessity and stern Reality. The fault? Quien sabe?

Throughout the night Smoke and his partner wheezed away at regular intervals with deep-seated coughs, swearing as they turned over from time to time. In the morning they turned out before I did. Smoke was a rather tall specimen, fairly well built, unshaven and unwashed, with lines not of weakness essentially, but of hardness with something of what is termed "criminality." He looked more like one who took his living from Society than one who trusted to Society's charity for it. As his partner packed in the morning and remarked on Smoke's lack of bedding, the latter said that he would "swipe" some soon. The partner looked to be of the other type, one who was an outcast thru weakness. Rather talkative he was, not, like Smoke, grimly silent except when it was necessary to say something. They left in opposite directions, agreeing to meet at the depot.

Wrote on some old boxes from 8 till 12. Squandered thirty-five cents (off my meal ticket) on "chicken pot pie" for lunch. Unlike the Holy Roman Empire, which was neither holy nor Roman, nor an Empire, this concoction had at least seen the inside of a pot.

In commenting later on his night with Smoke and his partner, Mills wrote, "I wish some of the complacent philosophers who believe in the justice and righteousness of 'Things as They Are' could feel even for a few days the sufferings some of these people live thru." The facetious tone that marked several of his early statements was gone by the time he wrote these words. His first days as an itinerant had created an awareness of the difficulty of life for seasonal workers that was to last the rest of his life.[13]

Sunday and Monday nights were easier for Mills, but they are still interesting because they show that he was learning how to live on the road. He no longer tried for respectable accommodations in a hotel or lodging house, nor did he attempt a search for a comfortable place to sleep. Instead he adopted the reasonable expedient of finding whatever was available close at hand. He was becoming an experienced hobo:

> May 25—6:30 P.M.
> Last night was Sunday night, but being neither in the clothes nor the mood to go to church I did the next best thing. "Cleanliness," saith the Good Book or some other book, "is next to Godliness." Godliness as far as I was concerned was impossible, so I betook myself to a wayside hydrant near town and performed such ablutions as were possible. Also rinsed out some of my dirty clothes. Felt like a fighting cock after getting some of the dirt off me.
> The night looked rather cloudy and after my experience of the previous night I sought a sheltered spot on the first throw. A long platform of Drake's packing house protected by an overhanging platform looked invitingly dry, tho hard. I slept fairly well, outside of the fact that I was punching orange-packers' cards all night. Got up at 5:30 and went to work at 6:30.

> May 27—(Wed.) 8:30 A.M.
> Monday night I had the first comfortable bed I had had since I started. We worked till nine o'clock, and after we had closed the boss heard me getting my roll of blankets from where I had tied them on the outside landing. "Where do you sleep, lad?" he said, when he saw who it was. He then told me I might sleep in the packing house that night, and suggested my using bundles of tissue wrapping paper as a bed.
> I took advantage of the opportunity to reach water by taking a bath at a running faucet in the packing house. I took my

outer clothing off for the first time in five days and lay down in Elysium on a paper bed. After twelve and one-half hours of hard physical work I slept like a top.

IV

After Tuesday's work, Mills judged it was time to move on. In an extended section in his journal he reflected upon his five days as a rustler and upon the effect of orange-packing work on the men and women he met:

May 27—(Wed.) 8:30 A.M.

This was the last day before pay-day and I felt that I had sufficiently investigated the inner workings of a packing house. I wanted, moreover, to look into the work of the pickers before I left Lindsay. I had worked five days as a "rustler." The work had been hard, naturally, but by this time I was hardened to it and could have kept the job longer. But time was pressing and I deemed I had learned all the job could teach me. I had come into close personal contact on fairly intimate terms with one of the great seasonal industries of the state. I had at least in a limited degree learned how they worked and felt and thought. The time had been short but it had enabled me to feel the pulse of another life than the one I had been living, a life not as far removed as some others I hope to come in contact with but sufficiently so for one to feel the essential difference.

Life for these people, at least during the working season, is hard. The easiest job in a packing house running from ten to twelve hours a day for six or seven days a week is enough to tax any man's endurance. Tho there is no strict discipline over the women, who are allowed to work pretty much when they care to, the fact that they all do piece work serves as a more stringent driving force than the rule of the strictest overseer. For 10 to 12 hours a day their flying hands repeat a monotonously mechanical movement. By closing time the girls are pale and worn looking, and I heard remarks time and again during the afternoon as to how tired they felt. Some of them are keeping house at the same time, so that after working at this terrific pace all day they must cook their own meals and presumably attend to the rest of their housework.

As to the men it cannot be said that their work is injurious, long tho the hours be. Combined, however, with periods of dissipation and unemployment, it undoubtedly tends toward an early destruction of their productive powers. Seasonal, temporary work of this character has as an inevitable concomitant these unemployed periods which consist, for many of the unmarried laborers, at least, of first a debauch, during which all their money is spent, then a period of tramping, undernourishment and all the accompanying ills until the next spell of work. This is not true of all, but from the conversations I have heard I know that it must be the case with many. Some of the men are older, married, with families. Their wives often work as packers in the same or similar packing houses. The total family income, then, is made up of this steady amount, secured during perhaps six months, and irregular sums secured intermittently during the rest of the year. This means for the entire family a fairly decent living during the working season, with what is likely to be excessive stringency during the rest of the year. Figures as to the number of families who live in this way are impossible to get but from the number of such cases in this district it is astonishingly large.

This sort of haphazard living, with the lack of conditions of steadiness, of predictability, with no possibility of providing for the future, and with periods of hard living for several months of each year, results inevitably in the lowering of the tone not only of the life of the family and the individual, but of the vitality of these economic and social units.

As to the women themselves it is difficult to draw conclusions from my limited observations. For the local people, working two or three months in the year probably does most of them no harm. The working conditions are clean and healthful apart from the long hours and the mechanical rigor of the work.

The independent single woman who follows this for a living, however, working six or seven months of the year at this and similar work is in a precarious or at least undesirable economic situation. It is possible for a skilled worker to earn enough during the complete working season to provide a fair living throughout the year. Whether or not they do so is a question. At best there must be a pressure with a constant temptation during the off seasons to augment their earnings by the same clandestine methods to which many of the shop girls of the cities are forced. The rigorous nature of their work while it lasts cannot but drain their strength unduly, tending to incapacitate them for the functions of motherhood.

There is little encouraging in this evaluation of working conditions in the orange industry. Perhaps the most telling remark that Mills made about the industry, however, appeared later in his journal:

May 27—(Wed.) 8:30 A.M.
    The conditions in this industry are perhaps the best that could exist in any seasonal industry. A certain number of workers, both men and women are assured of work for 5 or 6 months of the year. The work is skilled enough to prevent their inundation by the inflow of outside labor. Both men and women are employed so married life of a certain kind is possible.

If orange industry conditions were among the best that seasonal workers could expect, there was little reason to be optimistic about the typical life faced by the "tens, probably hundreds, of thousands" of seasonal workers Mills said existed in California. In reports he wrote after his trip, Mills claimed that where 4,600 people were employed in orange packing in the state during the period of peak activity; from 15,000 to 20,000 employees were needed each year between August 15 and December 1 to pick the grape crop; canneries required 15,000 workers for a limited period; and the lumber industry employed over 15,000 people in seasonal jobs. Carleton H. Parker estimated there were over 150,000 seasonal workers in the state. Mills left Lindsay so he could investigate what life was like for people in these other seasonal industries. He headed east to look for work in a Sierra lumber camp.[14]

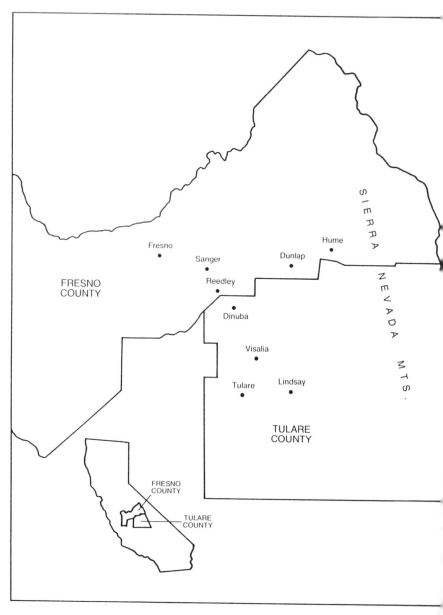

Map 3. Route of trip from Lindsay to Hume

3

Work in a Sierra
Lumber Camp

Hume, June 4th, 6 P.M.

Surrounded on three sides by high hills some 8,200 feet high, with snow still lying on their topmost points, Hume lies in a basin a mile or so long and one-half mile wide. Most of the basin is occupied by an artificial lake into which the great logs are dumped when cut. An enormous dam, built in successive arches, blocks the entrance to the basin. From this side the jagged backbone of the Sierra, snow-covered, seems but a short distance off. The well timbered sides of the basin, their desecration as yet incomplete, make the spot peculiarly attractive.

I

With these words, Mills described his arrival at a major lumbering area in the Sierra Nevada Mountains northeast of Lindsay.[1] He had noted early in his record that he wished to observe working conditions in the lumber industry, and his journal indicates that this plan met with the approval of Carleton H. Parker and the Immigration Commission. Leaving the orange-growing region around Lindsay, Mills walked and hitched rides west to Tulare and then north to Visalia (see Map 3). From there, he headed east toward the Sierras, traveling through Dinuba, Reedley, Sanger, and Dunlap as he moved toward the logging operations that he knew were underway at Hume. He arrived in Hume in the afternoon of June 4, 1914. For the next seven days he investigated the lumbering operation in the role of an unskilled itinerant. During his week at Hume, Mills learned all he felt he could as an employee about labor conditions at the camp. On June 11 he identified himself to officials of the Hume-Bennett Lumber Company, interviewed them to collect further information about conditions in the lumber industry, and left the Hume area to pursue other investigations in the Central Valley.

Several types of trees were abundant in the forests that blanketed the California coast and inland mountains, but the major source of timber in the area that Mills visited was the "giant tree," the sequoia redwood. Local histories indicate that the Hume camp was the final extension of redwood lumbering in the area. The first large-scale logging of sequoias was begun in the 1880s by the Smith-Moore Lumber Company at Millwood, west of Hume and at a lower elevation. Millwood prospered and grew through the 1890s, receiving publicity in the 1880s from the flume the company built, an impressive structure that snaked westward for fifty-four miles through forests and canyons to Sanger, Fresno County, where the company's main mill was located. When the Hume-Bennett Company bought Smith-Moore in 1907, it located its offices and storage yards in Sanger. The first major project of the new owners was to move the logging operation higher into the mountains to an altitude of 5,200 feet. A dam on Ten Mile Creek above the Millwood area created Hume Lake, and the Hume mill was built. Equipped with the best modern equipment, the new mill complex added a connection to the Millwood flume. Now more impressive than the original structure, the Hume flume was seventy-three miles long and touted as the longest and steepest in the world. As Mills reported to the Immigration Commission, "Three logging camps, the locations of which change from year to year, are situated in the adjoining mountains, from 4 to 8 miles from Hume. The timber, felled and cut into logs at the camps, is carried by train to an artificial lake at Hume. Here it is sawed at the mill, from which it is carried to Sanger in a . . . flume, the water being supplied from the lake."[2]

By the time Mills arrived in Hume in 1914, the state of California had built a road to the area. With easy access, Hume Lake later became a popular summer camping spot. Lumbering in the area ceased, however, only a few years after his trip. Because of the high cost of moving and processing the lumber, logging operations at Hume had never been profitable. When the mill burned down in 1917 it was not rebuilt. The remaining logs were removed over the next two years, and in 1919 logging stopped in the region. Fires in 1923 and 1928 destroyed most of the flume; later the surviving sections of the flume were dismantled to eliminate a fire hazard. Property in the area eventually reverted to the federal government and was included in the Sequoia National Forest.

II

Mills was aware of the lumber industry's current economic situation. He knew that 1914 was a low production year for the Hume-Bennett Lumber Company. Previous employment in the Hume complex had approached 500 men, but when he arrived it was only around 350. The reason for the low employment was that 1914 was a depression year in the United States. Mills found evidence of the depression in the hardships faced by many of the seasonal workers he met during his travels as an itinerant. His concern while at Hume was to discover how men in the logging industry dealt with the problems created by such irregular work.[3]

While walking to Hume, Mills passed through the recently abandoned camp at Millwood. His description of Millwood foreshadowed the fate in store for Hume:

Hume, June 4th, 6 P.M.

Millwood is the former site of the Hume-Bennett Co.'s lumber camp, from which they moved when the country around it was razed. A most desolate-looking place, with 20 to 30 deserted houses and stores, most of them still with stoves, tables, etc., in them. In one of the stores was a cash register. The framework necessary in a lumber camp lies haphazardly wrecked. A veritable city of the dead, a Pompeii from which the citizens have fled in a night. A small rippling stream runs thru the center of the ruins. One old man was crawling around in the wrecked camp like a ghoul in a graveyard. He pointed the Millwood trail out to me, a trail saving some seven miles of distance.

Mills understood that the scene at Millwood was one that was destined to be repeated at all logging camps that followed the practice of his time of cutting all trees of any size for a wide area around the camp. This future was still some way off at Hume, however. There was still much logging to do.

Soon after his arrival Mills began to look for a job. He asked several inhabitants of Hume for advice about where to apply for work. Based on their suggestions, the next day he traveled to one of the satellite camps surrounding Hume, where he succeeded in acquiring a job grading track for the company railroad. His job search was a typical one for an itinerant worker.

Hume, June 4th, 6 P.M.

Reached Hume at 3 P.M., ravenously hungry, having had nothing since breakfast. I finally persuaded a woman to break her afternoon siesta and cook me a meal. After getting a much-needed shave, to make me look less like a hobo and more like a working man, I looked the place over. . . .

Have heard that I may be able to get work in one of the construction camps here. Met an Italian boy coming from work who told me of it. . . .

I was directed to the timekeeper, an enormous whale of a man, who will get me a bunk, even tho I am not as yet working. . . .

Camp 6, Hume, June 5, 4:30 P.M.

The barber had previously told me that tho there had been a few too many men when the season opened, vacancies were constantly occurring. The timekeeper told me I had better try Camp 6, eight miles out, as there were no men wanted in the mill at Hume. He told me to take the "one-spot" out, train #1 of the two that ran out to the camps. . . .

Helped load wood onto the "one-spot," and we started off. The morning was very cold, it having snowed on some of the adjacent hills during the night. The little "one-spot" puffed up and up, always higher, winding around the side of the valley, revealing now and then wonderful views of the King's River Canyon and of the main Sierra range, jagged and snow-capped. There were three other passengers, two business men and the chunky Russian hobo I had seen at Hume. I struck up quite a conversation with him. . . . He got a job almost as soon as he arrived "bucking," that is, running a large cross-cut saw. His square Slavonian [sic] face was lit up with pleasure when I saw

him last. "Bucking" was the only job at which men were
needed, I was told, the camp being long-handed in other depart-
ments. Since this required considerable previous experience I
could not get on. However, I was referred to Mitchell, boss of
the "grading," or pick and shovel gang. He asked me if I had
been fired from another camp, then told me I was up against a
hard job, but could try it. I am told that he is a hard boss.

Had to take the "one-spot" back to Hume for my bed. Going
back with six heavily loaded cars, we jumped the track three
times, an "off again, on again" succession. . . .

Had a good lunch at Hume, bought a pair of overalls, and
came back on the "one-spot," helping to load her with wood
again. . . .

Tomorrow I become a toiler in this hive, absolutely unskilled,
selling a little physical strength for the sum of $2.25 a day, out
of which comes $.67 for meals. The work will be hard, but
"Lay on MacDuff, and damned be he that first cries 'Hold,
enough.' "

On June 6, Mills began work at Camp 6 of the Hume complex.
His report to the Immigration Commission contained a classification
of jobs in the camp and a general overview of the daily tasks:

The routine of the camp work may be briefly explained.
Under the supervision of the "Bucker boss," the trees are felled
by a pair of timber fallers, the limbs and, when necessary, the
bark removed by the limber and barkers, and the tree "bucked"
into logs of a uniform length by the cross-cutters. It then passes
into the hands of the yarding crew. Under the direction of the
"Logger" the riggers attach the rigging and the log is pulled by
the cable of a donkey engine to the required place for loading.
Here it is loaded upon a flat car by another crew with another
engine and carried to Hume to be sawed up. Of the general
force, the scaler measures and notes the number of feet in each
log shipped out—the barn-man attends to the horses and the
general sanitary conditions of the camp, while the "Donkey
Doctor" keeps the donkey engines in repair.[4]

The routine, technology, and size of the camp were typical of the
time that Mills wrote. Of the 350 men Mills estimated to be em-

The one-spot hauling lumber from the Converse mill to Millwood for drying and fluming to Sanger. Harold G. Schutt Collection, Department of Special Collections, Henry Madden Library, California State University, Fresno.

Bucking crew preparing a redwood log near Hume, California. Harold G. Schutt Collection, Department of Special Collections, Henry Madden Library, California State University, Fresno.

ployed in the complex, about 160 were employed in Hume at the mill, with the rest scattered among the three lumbering camps, at work on the company railroad, or at work constructing buildings in the camps. At Camp 6, where Mills was working, 53 men were employed in logging, 20 were extending the railroad, and 8 carpenters were working on camp buildings.[5]

In reading Mills's journal, it is easy to appreciate his reactions to a hard day's labor and his respect for the skill of the lumberjacks:

June 6th, 12:30 P.M.
Have just finished a half day's work on a grading gang, swinging mattock and shovel all morning. Air fine, work hard, but not man-killing. All rest of gang Greeks and Italians. We are making a grade upon which the camp Railroad can be extended. The work consists largely of filling in a cut with loose dirt.

June 6th, 7:30 P.M.
Put in a rather hard day, but feel fine now. Worked at pick and shovel work this A.M., but was put on a donkey-engine this afternoon, hauling water and wood to keep it going. A very audacious little engine, it pulls itself along a ways and then hauls great trees hither and thither. . . .
The grading gang at work is most interesting. I am the only English-speaking one among them. This is the lowest and most unskilled form of work in the camp. For ten hours a day we swing a pick, mattock, or shovel dirt. Monotonously the same, it is the kind of work requiring a strong back and a weak mind, if ever there were such work. While the boss is around the men swing regularly away, saying but little. Mitchell is the foreman's name, a red-faced Irishman who has the reputation of being a slave-driver. . . . So far he has been mild and pleasant to me. When he is gone for a few minutes the sons of Sparta and Athens, descendants of heroes of Salamis and of Marathon, together with the children of Imperial Rome, let forth a flood of melodious language, passing jokes back and forth, leaning on their shovels and picks.

June 11, 7:30 A.M.
Finished work as pick- and shovel-handler last night, so have a little time to catch up on back notes.

Most of my work during the last five days has been the monotonous swinging of pick, shovel, or mattock. Ten hours a day we swing our arms in a certain uniform fashion, almost unceasingly. One gets the regular "navvy" swing in time. The shovel placed in the dirt, a slight pause, the pressure of foot or knee, another pause, shovel loosened, backward step with foot, shovel swung around with turn of body in a rhythmic swing, upper hand slid along handle, and dirt is thrown 15 or 20 feet; and repeat ad infinitum.

On Monday, while shoveling, a pile of loose dirt on a rock invited my shovel and I thrust it in unearthing, rather violently, a charge of dynamite. If I had chanced to strike a cap ———?

Monday afternoon the monotony of the work was a little broken thru my being put to assist the blacksmith in putting up a tent. My work consisted largely in dragging around heavy timbers, but at that it was a relief from the gang work. . . .

The next afternoon Widdy [the camp boss] put me at work grading a bed for a giant redwood. . . . I was enabled at this work to get a better idea of the work in the woods proper. Our task consisted in grading off a level bed in which the tree should fall when felled. The first four logs in a giant redwood are worth about $200 each while the whole tree is worth from $1,200 to $1,500. Hence the extreme importance of not breaking it. The need of highly skilled timber-fellers is evident, for redwoods in particular are easily broken.

The work of the timber-fellers is an art in itself. Mostly Swedes, and young, they are a powerful set of men. Two of them work together on a tree. First the under-cut is made, a deep cut on the side to which the tree is to fall. This is done with axes, and how the chips do fly! Systematically they attack the largest trees, and in an incredibly short space of time it is cut half thru. As I watched them, a great sap stream was struck, gushing out as water does from a garden hose, gallons and gallons of it. Then the tree is sawed from the other side, and by regulating this, and the proper placement of the under-cut, the direction of the fall is controlled. Almost invariably, even tho it be windy, the tree can be dropped just where it is wanted. It is said that these men can drive a stake with the top of a tree 9 times out of 10. The tree I was working on was dropped between two saplings the distance between which just equalled the width of the tree.

When the tree is about ready to fall the fallers send out a ringing melodious cry as a warning, something almost like a yodel. Just as it starts to fall this is repeated. Then comes the roar, the crash, the great thud as the monster sways and falls, often taking with it 5 or 6 trees which are themselves giants, but pygmies as compared with it. With several sets of fallers working in the woods, the melodious halloos echoing thru the woody canyons, followed by the thunderous crashes, form a constant succession of sound, as the forest recedes before the advance of man.

In Hume, as he had in Lindsay, Mills paid particular attention to the people with whom he worked. Two of the more colorful characters he encountered were a Russian he first met at Sanger while on his way to Hume and his tent-mate Tony, an Italian laborer:

Another brother of the road soon trudged up, a type foreign to any I had previously met. . . . He was a Russian, about thirty years old, and had come to America five years ago. Having no regular trade, he had worked as a fireman on a boat running to South America for about a year, and then had worked as a cross-cutter in the Canadian lumber camps. After a period of this he had worked on a life-saving crew in Louisiana. In March of this year, he had come from New Orleans to Los Angeles, hoboing 2,000 miles in 15 days. Since then he had worked at odd jobs for a few days at a time. He spoke bitterly of conditions here, saying that he had been told there was plenty of work and yet he could get nothing to do. In his broken English he told how the Los Angeles employment agencies charged a man $2 for a job that would last but a day or so. His last job had been in Mendocino County, where he had worked 18 days in a railroad construction camp, leaving, he said, because the pay was too poor. There were too many men on the road here, and he planned to go to Utah, near Salt Lake City, where he had heard there was plenty to do. This man undoubtedly was really and earnestly after work. His simple hazel eyes almost filled with tears as he told of the hard times and the difficulty of getting work. Strong, sturdy, simple-minded and good-hearted, in the place he had heard of as the land of milk and honey, there seemed to be none for him. By chance I saw him later applying for work at Hume, and when he was given a place as a "bucker," his broad face lit up like that of a child.[6]

Tony, Mills's tent-mate, was younger than the Russian and had yet to become discouraged by life as a casual worker. Mills worked with Tony on the grading crew most of the time during his stay at the lumber camp. He wrote about the Italian frequently in his journal and added the following longer statement about Tony's background in his report "Scenes and Incidents 'On the Road' ":

> Antonio Frau, or "Tony" as he told me to call him, was a fellow worker in the grading crew at Hume. Twenty-three years old, he was born in the Island of Sardinia. Short but stockily built, brown-faced, black-haired, black-mustached, with sparkling black eyes, he was a typical son of sunny Italy. One of a family of four children, he was raised on a small farm. One can make there about 60 cents a day, according to Tony, but there is no chance to save money. So five years ago, when he was 18 years old, Tony came to New York. For one year he worked around New York state, returning home at the end of that time. He had made $250, but his round trip having cost him $160, his net earnings were $90. He stayed in Sardinia for three years, and then took a trip to Panama, where he worked for a considerable period with a construction crew and returned home again. Fourteen months ago Tony, this time with a brother, came again to New York, leaving a married and an unmarried sister at home with their widowed mother. For 12 months he stayed near New York working on bridge-building, tunnel-work, road-building, railroad construction, etc., making from $2.25 to $2.75 a day. Hearing wonderful tales of the amount of work and the high wages in California, Tony came out last March, leaving his brother in New York. For two months he stayed in San Francisco and could get no work. Finally a friend wrote him that he could get work at Hume, and with two others he came, having worked here now for one month and saved $45.
>   Tony is unmarried, and says that practically all Italians who work as he does from place to place are also unmarried, as a

settled life is impossible. He likes this country and believes that English and American people are all right. Remembering, doubtless, experiences with traction foremen, he thinks little of the Irish, who "Make work like Hell" says Tony.

His ambition is to save enough to get a small farm or store, bring out a wife from Italy and settle down. Tho some Italians go back to Italy, he does not plan to return again. Most Italians have similar plans for the future and generally get away from this life by the time they are 35 or at latest, 40. This accounts for the marked preponderance of relatively young Italians on work of this kind.[7]

Tony represented a different class of migrant worker than the Russian. He had definite reasons for doing the work he was doing, and he had plans for getting out of itinerant life. Tony also provided an excellent example of contemporary Italian immigrants to the United States. Italians traveled throughout the Western hemisphere in search of work, often to return later to their native land. In the pre–World War I period, over half of the immigrants to the United States from Italy returned home. The social and economic opportunities available were the main determinants of their work patterns. Recent comparisons of Italian migration to the United States and Argentina have found that those coming to the United States tended to be young, single, unskilled males. They were attracted by the high wages in U.S. urban areas and intended to return to Italy. Immigrants to Argentina, on the other hand, tended to be skilled or professional workers who intended to stay. With a larger and longer-settled Italian population, Argentina was more attractive to permanent immigrants. Tony fit perfectly the picture of the typical Italian immigrant to the United States.[8]

Although he did not describe other people at length, Mills did write short accounts in his journal about the men he met on the "one-spot" traveling to Camp 6 and about several others at the camp:

Camp 6, Hume, June 5, 4:30 P.M.

Two men rode back on the train who had just given up jobs such as I am to start, saying that the work was so hard they could not sleep. Both were past middle age, with hardened veins, and the look of men who could not stand heavy work. Both had been up for a month. One was an engine-man usually. Had done some of that work here, then had been put to drilling, and had graded for 2 days. He did not know where he was going, but said he could get another job. He had been told that if he would stay a day or so he could get an engine-job, but he did not intend to do so. Had worked last summer in a mill at Portersville. He said that Italians and Greeks were driving the white men out, because they would work harder and could be driven by the bosses, cursed, etc. Stated that the Mexicans would not work as these two races would.

June 6th, 7:30 P.M.

Had a talk with the engineer in charge, after quitting. He is called the "Donkey-Doctor," being the mechanic in general charge of the repairing of all donkeys out of order. Formerly in the oil fields, this is his second winter at this game.

There are 65 men in this camp, and five donkey engines at present. There are about 400 men in the whole place. Last year 600–700, he says. . . .

Engineer says that little of [the] work requires great skill. New men are put at almost all jobs, tho old men are given preference. Many men here come back each year, tho there are always many new men, especially at rough work.

Engineer says he thinks many of the men are farmers in the interim, but this is doubtful. I must find out what they do in the off-season. One, I know, is an upholsterer by trade. He came into our tent tonight for some hay with which to make himself a bed. He had walked from Sanger. At Millwood he had left his blankets by the roadside a minute. An auto had come along; the driver had thought the roll was lost and carried it back to Sanger. A more fiendish turn of fate could hardly be imagined.

June 11, 7:30 A.M.

The youthful appearance of a young Italian in the construction gang prompted me to inquire about him. I found that he is but 19 years old and has been doing such work since he was 16. His family live[s] somewhere in the East on a farm, but he has struck out for himself. Slight of build, he appears to be but a baby among the brawny bunch with which he works, but he holds up his end.

Monday evening at supper a remark, directed at the young man in charge of the donkey who had helped me get fixed, concerning "college chums" impelled me to sound him a little as to what he did in the off-season. He had been going to school, he said. When I asked him where, he said "Berkeley," and when I asked what class he said he had just graduated. "Hell," said I, "so did I." At which it developed that he had recognized me when I first arrived. I felt compelled to explain my work to him. Working in the grading gang, he explained, would not bring me at all into touch with the lumber-men and woodsmen. He offered, therefore, to explain the situation to Widdy. Tho averse to doing so, I saw that it was the only method possible to get the contact with the men I wanted to meet.

June 11, 7:30 A.M.

The floating element is also made up almost entirely of men without family ties. Most of these are older men 35 to 45 or even 50. A few are married, however. A small man came up two days ago and asked Mitchell if he could use a good man. He was taken on, and came to work yesterday. Before I had talked to him 5 minutes he had mentioned three or four times that he had a wife and six children at Long Beach, a second wife, by the way. I later heard him give the boss the same information. "Marrying is an awful responsibility for a man," he said. Some one asked him why he had come so far for a job. "Why," he said, "if you had a wife and six children to support you'd go to Hell for a job." Some I have met . . . would go to Hell to avoid getting a job.

Dan, as he told the boss to call him, was a follower of the elusive goddess of invention. He had a plan that would enable every soul on a sinking ship to get off in 30 seconds. He had written to Roosevelt about it, why I don't know, except that Roosevelt was "a dare-devil," according to Dan. As soon as he got on his feet he was to have it patented. He hinted that there was a chance for a clever, intelligent, honest, capable man of unimpeachable integrity to join him in the enterprise and make big money and fame. I could not recognize all the qualities as being mine, and could not enthuse. Doubtless a small investment was required.

Two other of the floating type have come into my tent, and Tony has moved. They are young men, about 27 to 30, one with a wife he has not visited for six months. They left Mexical, where they have been knocking around at odd jobs, two weeks ago, with $200. They are now "broke." The married one states that he is an electrical engineer, but they came here to get any jobs they could get. The engineer is a man of consummate nerve. He told Widdy that he could take any job in camp, tho he knew little about any of the work. His nerve stayed with him, however, and he got away with his job of spool-tender. He told me of how he had got a job tending a gasoline engine on Tulare Lake. Applying for a job, he was asked if he could run such an engine. "Hell, yes." (He had never laid a finger on one before.) He was sent down to it, found out from a person living near how it was started, and when his boss came around he had a great stream of water pumping out. Before the boss came back again, two weeks later, he had learned all about it. Consummate nerve plus consummate ability at lying appear to take a man a long way in some lines.

In addition to describing the people he met, Mills also had much to say about the daily life of the camp. He described living conditions several times in his journal and recounted incidents that showed how individuals spent their spare time. Ranging from accounts of fights between workers to tales of snipe hunts in the woods, these descriptions completed his observations of the daily life of the men in the industry:

Dunlap, June 4, 8 A.M.
    Met a white-shirted figure hobbling wearily down the road in the darkness. We stopped, and he sat down anxious to talk. He was evidently very lonely, and had something on his mind he was anxious to talk about. I sat down with him. He lit a cigarette, the flame revealing a pale white face, tired, with rather watery gray eyes, yet not a weak face.
    He had been third cook at Camp Three at Hume, and had lost his job because he had had a fight. And what a fight it had been! With a delightful Southern drawl in his voice he told me of it. The rags with which he used to open the hot oven door had been taken as fast as he got them. When they were gone he burned his fingers every time he opened the door. Finally he cut the corners off his own rags: ten minutes later he found one in

the possession of a camp "flunkey." The cook took possession forcibly. "You've got your nerve," said the "flunkey." "You're God damned right I've got my nerve," said the cook. Whereat the flunkey started round the table towards him. The cook met him half way, closed one of his eyes, pummeled him around the room and finally knocked him down. Tho rebuked by the chief cook nothing was done. The next morning, entering the room as the flunkey was sweeping, the latter swung the broom handle against his head. "And this time I sure did finish him," said the cook. Finally the flunkey grabbed a 12-inch butcher knife and made a rush for him. The cook swung to his jaw and turned him clean around, grabbing his wrist as he did so. The flunkey changed hands with the knife and struck for his head. Dodging, he grabbed the other wrist and brought it down, "just twisted hell out of it," throwing the knife to the end of the room. Both were fired. Instead of the $65 a month which the cook had been promised, he was paid $60. He was headed for Fresno when I met him.

June 6th, 7:30 P.M.

Three times a day we come in to feed. Unwashed, most of us, we pour in: animals we come to satisfy an animal desire. We come to feed and conceal it not by the furbishings and amenities of a polite civilization. The veneer is thin here. Three tables, 20 at a table, we eat, we stoke the human furnace.

The faces are not the dissolute, shiftless type I saw predominate in the orange picking and among the hoboes. Faces unshaven, often unwashed, but strong with the lines of strong men. No one type predominates. The men are of many shades and many tongues. But none are the "pampered products of a petted civilization." All are strong, self-reliant, engaged in a man's sized job.

The men are not merely vicious, or vulgarly profane. When they swear they swear roundly, but not with the refined obscenities I heard among the hoboes and orange workers. A much cleaner, more wholesome class of men.

The workers live in tents and cabins, about four together. There are no toilets (Now are), the hill-sides nearby being used.

The water used seems to be piped from a distance, so little danger, tho such a method is unclean.

The weather is very cold. Water freezes if it is not running. There was a little touch of snow at 5 P.M. today. There is but little sun all day, as the work is carried on in the great canyons of shade made by the giant trees.

June 11, 7:30 A.M.

The technical vernacular of a logging camp is most interesting. The terms applied to various things, cables, runways, etc. are brightly imaginative and picturesque, tho unprintable.

I was brought into contact with an old lumber jack, who is in charge of the falling and sawing of the trees. One Jake Olsen, a Swede about 45 years old, intelligent as most lumber-jacks are, he is the life of the camp with his laughter and witticisms. Speaking with a slight accent, he is constantly "joshing" everyone in camp. The great joke they have on Jake occurred two years ago. A green boy, somewhat fresh, came up, was taken "snipe-hunting" and was almost lost in the woods. Inspired by the others, the boy then tried to play the trick on Jake, the oldest man in the woods. The delight of the camp may be imagined.

Mills's observations of daily life in Hume are consistent with other reports of life in logging camps. The silence when eating, the masses of food consumed, the fights, the swearing, the jokes, and the sleeping accommodations were standard fare. In many logging camps, men were crammed into bunkhouses and given inadequate sanitation facilities. At Hume, however, Mills found conditions to be generally satisfactory. There was a company store near the mill, but its operation raised no objections. No one complained about the quality or cost of the food provided in the cook house either. Sanitation facilities at Camp 6 were inadequate, but permanent facilities were being built when Mills was there, and sanitation was satisfactory at the Hume complex.

Wages at the camp were high enough that workers were not permanently in debt to the company for supplies or room and board. Mills estimated that workers cleared per month, after all obligations to the company, from $38.50 (for grading hands, section hands, and wood-buckers) to $100 (for loggers, donkey doctors, and the chief cook). He estimated that the average worker left Hume with $300 to $350 at the end of the season. This was an enormous sum compared to the $30 that Carleton H. Parker estimated was the average "winter stake" that seasonal workers had in hand to face the winter months of unemployment.[9]

III

Based on these observations, Mills drew several conclusions about work in the logging industry. The first feature of camp work that he identified was the division of labor by nationality. Mills was the only native English-speaking person on his grading crew. The others were all from Italy or Greece. He commented in his report to the Immigration Commission:

> The common large tent into which the men crowd at meal times contains a most cosmopolitan assemblage of types and races, being a veritable melting pot. The types, however, are fairly well separated in the work they do.
>
> The work in the woods is almost exclusively in the hands of what might be termed the Northern type, the American, German and Swede predominating. Practically all of the work of timber falling, the swinging of the axe, is done, strangely enough, by Swedes, while much of the slow, patient work of sawing is done by Germans, tho both these types are seen at other work as well. A large proportion of the working force are, of course, Americans, many of the pure stock of New England and Kentucky being found in the woods. Several Scotchmen, three Italians, and two Russians are included in the force of the logging camp proper. These Italians, it is interesting to note, are the only ones out of hundreds that have been tried, that have shown an ability to do independent, responsible work.
>
> The construction crew are a mixed lot of Scotch, Irish and American casuals, with several Greeks and Italians. The grading crew, the lowest class of unskilled workers, consists of five Greeks, one Italian, and two Americans. . . .
>
> All of the workers in the camp, concerning whom I was able to get any information, including the Swedes and the Germans,

were citizens, with the exception of the Greeks, Italians and Russians, none of whom appear to have become naturalized. Of the Swedes and Germans, none are recent arrivals in this country, while none of the Greeks or Italians are as yet able to speak English with any degree of perfection.[10]

In addition to the division of work by nationalities, Mills concluded that there was another important distinction in camp between permanent and temporary workers. The logging itself tended to be done by stable workers, while construction and maintenance tended to be done by the floating class. He estimated that 70 percent of the jobs in the camp required some skill or experience. Most men in these positions came back to the camp yearly and stayed for the season. A small proportion of experienced men and almost all those with unskilled jobs only stayed for a short time and then moved on. Almost all the workers who quit while he was in the camp had unskilled jobs. Mills estimated that approximately half of the workers at any one time were stable employees and that the other half belonged to the floating class. The turnover in logging camps was notorious, and it has been commented on by many historians of the lumber industry. Mills's analysis suggests the important qualification that turnover was concentrated among specific groups of workers.[11]

The difference between floating and stable workers was also evident in the attitudes and actions of the men. Mills commented on them in his journal:

June 11, 7:30 A.M.

These woodsmen, the "lumber-jacks," are a type unto themselves. Tho the camp here is decidedly cosmopolitan in character, a melting pot of types and races, the skilled woodsmen form an exclusive little body, with their own traditions and interests. As compared with the unskilled men of the camp they occupy a position similar, or superior, to that occupied by the skilled artisans of the city as compared to the laborers. Men who handle thousands of dollars worth of property a day, a single slip perhaps meaning a severe loss, men who have lived in the woods all their lives, with the pride of knowledge and skill, they rank among the aristocracy of labor. Often your true woodsman will not work at anything else during the off-season of some five or

six months. Earning a goodly "stake," the older men live on it
thru the winter. . . .

The flotsam and jetsam of the labor market, the floating
laborers, are, of course, represented here. They work in the grading and construction gangs, [and] they do some "bucking" and
other work requiring little skill or experience. In general they
are cordially despised by the woodsmen. Few of them stay for
any length of time, and practically none come back the next season. (There have been one or two striking exceptions to this.)
The woodsmen almost invariably stay the season thru, and most
of them return to the same camp each succeeding year. Some of
the best men sign up for the following season at the close of
each year. . . . The real woodsman can get a place at any time
during the season. Usually men obtained thru employment
agencies, "Rough and Ready" men, are of little value as woodsmen.

With lines drawn between national groups and between stable and
floating workers, the lumber camp workforce was not as unified a
group of laborers as might appear at first glance. Mills discovered,
however, that some features of the work affected all workers the same
way. For example, all the workers had to adjust their lives to the
seasonal nature of the industry. He summarized the nature of the
problem in his report:

Tho lumbering is one of the most stable of the seasonal
industries, a demand such as this, extending over a period of six
or seven months of the year, has the same general effect upon
the character of our labor force as an industry having a season
of but two or three months. It means the existence of a reserve
labor force either idle and unproductive, or only intermittently
and ineffectively productive for five months of the year, or 40%
of the time. It involves the essential impossibility of marriage
and a settled life for a very considerable portion of our labor
population.[12]

Most men in the logging camp were unmarried. The absence of a
normal family life for the vast majority of lumber workers was a fact
that transcended differences in skill, nationality, or job group. Another similarity was the young age of most of the men in the camp.
Mills estimated the range of their ages in his report:[13]

The ages of the actual workers run from nineteen to about
forty, tho a few foremen, etc. would exceed the latter age. By far
the greater proportion are between twenty-five and thirty-five.
The reason for this is not far to seek. The work among the
woodsmen proper is of the sort that demands the strength of a
young man. Swinging an axe or running a sixteen-foot saw for
ten hours a day is not work for one who is past his prime. . . .
The ages of the men in the grading and construction crews
would run a little higher, but this also is work that a man over
forty cannot stand. Your casual laborer beyond that age is
become a habitué of city streets and alleys, trusting to the odd
jobs that bring in a quarter or so for a livelihood.[14]

Mills also noted the absence of mental stimulation in the camp.
Physically the work was healthful, but exercise was all it offered.
Mills discussed the problem in a striking passage in his journal:

June 11, 7:30 A.M.
    Mechanical physical work such as I have been doing, requir-
ing no mental effort of any kind, is the most deadening life I
have experienced. Ten hours a day I try to give my mind something to do. All the long, weary morning, all the dreary waste
of the afternoon, one's mind is ceaselessly seeking some pabu-
lum to digest. Hard thinking on any subject I find impossible
with the work. I think over snatches of poetry; I hum tunes;
but there is no escape from the dreary vacuity. The physical
work is endurable, yea, not even disagreeable when one gets
used to it, but the mental sterility accompanying such work is
unendurable. How the other workers stand it I do not know. . . .
    The men here, tho intelligent, have a markedly narrow range
of interests. Talk of common camp interests, of each time a certain hot-tempered individual throws his hat down and jumps on
it, etc., almost exhausts their topics of conversation. Few of
them read at all, so time not spent in working is drearily heavy
on their hands. The life they live, the life I have led for a week
or so here, is a splendid one as a perfect type of animal existence. The regular working, eating, sleeping, the wonderful cli-
mate (of late the weather has been super-glorious, cold mornings
with a "kick" to them, warm days, yet never suffocatingly hot,
cool, clear nights) allow a man to live the perfect physical life.

Every organ functions perfectly. Heart, lungs, stomach work as well-oiled machinery. Food tastes like ambrosia. Sleep in the rough cots is a virtual "Paradisa Gloria." Yet drearily empty it all is, after all. More satisfactory would it be if a man had a blank where his mind is. Better fifty years of soul-satisfying, mentally stimulating existence than a cycle of mere bodily existence, perfect tho it be.

Of the features common to all work in the industry, Mills thought that the most damaging to the character of the men was the seasonality of the work. The long periods where a steady income could not be counted on created temptations that often led to dissolution. Mills commented at length on these temptations in his report:

The off-season in this industry runs from October till the latter part of April, a period of from five to six months. The lumber-jacks may be divided into two classes, according to the disposition they make of the money they have earned and according to what they do during this period. On the one hand we have most of the younger men and some of the older ones as well, who are still unsettled in character. Leaving camp with a large "stake," larger than that obtainable in almost any other seasonal industry, they head for the nearest "live" town, or possibly for some of the larger cities. There follows a period of more or less riotous dissipation, lasting for from several days to several weeks, ending when their "stake" is gone. This is looked forward to by a large percentage of them as the natural way to spend their money. Their general attitude is expressed by a common joke among them that lumber-jacks invest their money in winter in "houses and lots"—houses of prostitution and lots of whiskey. The men then live thru the three or four lean months of winter as best they can, doing what odd work they can pick up. Few of them, however, descend to the condition of being a mere "bum." . . .

The evil effects of a life of this nature is [sic] ultimately felt by these men, strong type tho they be. The vicious alternation of hard work and dissipation tend toward an early destruction of their productive powers if long continued.

On the other hand there is here a large representation of the steadier and more sober worker, the men over thirty usually having passed thru this stage of winter dissipation. Most of these men, intelligent and with a pride in their work, do not care to take the odd jobs they can pick up in the off-season. The money they have saved will support them in good style during this period, with usually something over. The steadier men lay away this surplus, many of them planning to get out of the lumber work within a few years. This class generally leave before they are over thirty-five or forty, purchasing a ranch and settling down. Some of them become foremen and camp bosses, these positions always being filled by men who have received the training of an ordinary wood-jack. All of them, however, do not end up in this way, a considerable proportion drifting into the army of casual "floaters," later to become the social derelict to which this life inevitably leads. In a recent collection of unemployed, the woods boss at Hume counted three of the best woodsmen he had ever had, sunk to the lowest grade of casual worker.[15]

Despite the serious problems created by seasonality, Mills concluded that workers in the lumber industry had an advantage over those in other seasonal industries. They had a chance, however slim it might be, to escape the casual labor cycle:

In one respect it is worthy of note, lumbering differs from almost every industry in which casual work is offered. The most discouraging fact in the life of a member of this "reserve army" of labor, is that after one has become a casual worker it is almost impossible to break away from this life. The jobs one gets thru employment agencies, those one hears of thru one's associates, are temporary jobs. It is almost impossible for the casual worker to get anything approaching steady work. The foot-hold, then, that one requires to escape from the life can seldom be obtained. Even if one desires to save the large "stake" that means escape, as the younger members of this labor force, who have not yet been thoroughly impregnated with the virulent disease of "casuality," often do, the opportunity is not given. But this industry does give it. In such a camp as this, money cannot be spent during the season. If a man does satisfactory work, he is sure of a job all season and usually the next season, too, if he cares to come back. The "stake" that means independence can be saved. And tho 75% or 80% of the casual workers are past redemption in this regard, many find this to afford the way out. The places open at first are neither easy nor extremely plentiful, but there are usually chances for a man to get his start in the construction crews or in the mill. Several men were pointed out to me who, first striking a stray job in camp, held it and have come back for several years, getting better jobs all the time. Tho seasonal in its nature, with many of the faults that characterize all such industries, lumbering has a social value in this respect that is of not inconsiderable importance in regard to the problems in hand.[16]

At the beginning of this statement, Mills described a situation that has come to be recognized as an important characteristic of labor markets—the problem of secondary workers in a dual labor market economy. These terms would not have been familiar to Mills, but he would have recognized the concepts behind them. In effect two labor markets existed in California, one for permanent workers and one for temporary workers, with little overlap. Once workers acquired a history of temporary and unskilled employment they had little chance of being hired for permanent jobs. His recognition of the dual labor market trap of casual labor shows a keen insight into the nature of the seasonal industries he was investigating. The situation faced by the Russian itinerant, who wanted stable work but was not able to get it, becomes understandable in this frame of analysis.[17]

Mills's claim that lumbering provided conditions allowing workers to leave seasonal work is also an important point. The workers he met in the orange industry did not have this opportunity. He concluded that orange packers were well off in terms of seasonal work because the skill required allowed decent wages and because the location of the work allowed a family life, but orange packers did not earn enough to break out of the seasonal cycle. Thus, in his view, workers in the lumber industry were perhaps the most favorably situated of all seasonal workers in California.

It is possible to make an estimate of the relative size of this favored group by using data gathered during the Immigration Commission's investigations. Of the 150,000 seasonal workers Parker claimed existed in California, Mills estimated that 30,000 were employed in the lumber industry, with about half of these in seasonal jobs. If he was correct in his analysis, then only a small fraction of the seasonal labor population had a good opportunity to escape from the seasonal cycle.[18]

No specific recommendations were made in Mills's report to the Immigration Commission for policies to change conditions in the lumber industry. The statewide programs begun by the Immigration Commission—particularly those of itinerant education and labor camp inspections—did improve camp living conditions. In the short time period before World War I that public attention was focused on itinerant problems, however, nothing was done that fundamentally changed the nature of the industry. Logging industry workers continued to live and work much as Mills described far into the years ahead.

4

The Employment
Agency Game

Reedley. June 14th. 1914.

The situation is very bad whether Ball is in league with the
employment agent or not. Men have been sent up in droves,
with the certainty that they will not hold the job. Lured by
short hours, unsuspecting foreigners pay their fees and fare,
only to last a day or so.

It is claimed that they cannot do the work, but yet the same
sort of men (all foreigners, Hindus, Armenians, Mexicans, etc.)
are still sent up. If not crooked, tho all appearances indicate
that certain employment agencies & auto firms are reaping a
harvest (or have been), it is a most absurdly inefficient way of
obtaining labor.

I

Mills used these words to comment on the situation at a road
construction project he investigated after leaving Hume.[1] California
was the scene of intensive railroad and highway building, and he
decided early in his journey to look into employment practices in
the industry. The roadwork Mills investigated was taking place on
the Sand Creek Road just south of the General Grant National Park
in Tulare and Fresno counties. Different contractors had responsibility for the work in the two counties, and Mills visited both labor
camps. He wrote a report for the Immigration Commission on "The
Sand Creek Road Situation" in addition to his usual notes and journal
entries.[2]

Mills found very different conditions in the two labor camps. The Tulare County project employed two eight-man crews made up entirely of "the American type, reliable, efficient workmen." Working and living conditions were satisfactory. The Fresno County camp, however, was very different. The single crew utilized was comprised totally of foreigners, the men lived under dreadful conditions, and the work was far behind schedule. Mills suspected, but was not able to prove, that the contractor for the Fresno County work, Ball, was using the employment agency game, a particularly vicious scheme used to exploit itinerant workers. It involved an employment agency in town sending men to a job if they paid a fee to the employment agency and a fee for the transportation. The contractor, who was part of the scam and took a share of the fees, would force the workers out after they had earned little or nothing by making working conditions so bad as to be unendurable or by firing the workers on a contrived pretense.

Ball hired all his workers through employment agencies in Fresno and transported them to the construction camp by truck. The agency charged the workers a one-dollar fee for the job and three dollars for the forty-mile trip. Mills found that as many as fifteen to twenty men arrived each day for a work crew that averaged twenty when work was at its peak. He estimated that hundreds of workers had made the trip to Ball's camp in the three months before his investigation.

The employment agency game was illegal, and employers knew it. Because Mills was unable to prove that the scheme was being used on the Sand Creek Road, he was cautious in his report to the Immigration Commission in order to avoid making false claims about Ball's operation. But he did go so far as to say that a severe exploitation of itinerants was occurring, and he also implied that the employment agencies and contractor knew what they were doing.

Other investigators of labor market conditions shared Mills's concern about employment agency practices. Both the U.S. Industrial Relations Commission and the California Immigration Commission looked into the matter. Carleton H. Parker took up the question in a "Preliminary Report on Tentative Findings and Conclusions in the Investigation of Seasonal, Migratory and Unskilled Labor in California," which he submitted to the Industrial Relations Commission on September 1, 1914. Basing his conclusions on reports from investigators he sent out to survey employment agencies, Parker found that only three public employment agencies operated in the state, all at the municipal level. The state government was not involved in job placement. Among the three municipal agencies that were involved—in Sacramento, Berkeley, and Los Angeles—there was no cooperation at all, and commission investigators found the agencies to be ineffective and inefficient. In the private market in California, some 350 agencies existed, most in San Francisco and Los Angeles. Based on reports from his agents, Parker drew several conclusions about the private sector.[3]

1. There was no cooperation between private agencies. They made their money from employment fees and thus did not refer men to other agencies in the area or in other cities.

2. Fees varied according to the state of the labor market and the apparent financial circumstances of job applicants. Fees were higher in winter and during depressions, and they were higher for workers who were well dressed. Parker knew of instances of different fees being charged for the same job.

3. It was almost always the case that the supply of applicants was greater than the number of jobs available. This had been particularly true just before completion of the investigation during the recession period from mid-1913 to mid-1914.

4. Parker asserted that "there is considerable evidence of fraud on the part of private employment agents." He found that itinerants referred to employment agents as "labor sharks" and, if at all possible, avoided going to the agencies. Moreover, job applicants were constantly misinformed about the nature of jobs available; workers were at times charged hospital fees even though they stayed with a job for only a few days; and there was a "probability" of collusion between employers and agents in terms of fee splitting, leading to intentional rapid turnover of work crews.

5. Because of the poor reputation of private employment agencies, Parker found that most job placement took place through other sources. He mentioned hotelkeepers and saloonkeepers, and he found in one small agricultural town that a local saloon placed more men in one day than the private employment agency placed in a month.

When Parker's report—and others like it by investigators in other parts of the United States—were submitted to the Industrial Relations Commission, the commission concluded that private employment agencies were one of the major causes of a chaotic seasonal and itinerant labor market. In a report summarizing information collected from all over the country, William Leiserson, a principal investigator for the Industrial Relations Commission, concluded that "instead of relieving unemployment and reducing irregularity, these employment agencies actually serve to congest the labor market and to increase idleness and irregularity of employment." Leiserson listed the same types of frauds as Parker had and claimed (giving several examples from states other than California) that fraud was common across the United States. Leiserson felt that many private employment agents were honest, but he noted that the reputation of employment agencies was so bad that honest agents often left the industry after a short time. Leiserson saw no simple legislative solution to these problems. He believed that little could be done other than to outlaw dishonest agencies, but pointed out that this had already been accomplished in the vast majority of states.[4]

II

Frederick Mills described the exploitation of itinerants by the employment agency game in the draft of a novel he began in the 1950s. After suffering a heart attack in 1953, Mills devoted much of his spare time for several months to reviewing his "hobo" records and drafting a short novel of about 150 double-spaced pages, which has survived among his papers. The main part of the story recounts, in a slightly reorganized chronology, almost all the experiences he had on his trip. It follows the adventures of two young itinerants from the East, Ben (who represents Mills) and Red. Mills used the format of a novel effectively to present his views on the life he saw and on the difficulties he knew existed in resolving the problems faced by itinerant workers.[5]

Mills's novel allowed him to comment on his experiences in a way that was not possible in his other writings. For example, his fictional account of his trip to the Sand Creek Road gang is a particularly apt summary of the employment agency game. In a lengthy section, Mills tells about Ben's experiences after he has quit his job as a rustler in a Lindsay orange packinghouse and is wandering between towns in the Tulare County area. He learns about work on the Sand Creek Road when he goes to an employment agency in Fresno to get a job:

During the several days following Ben wandered through the country, jungling at Visalia, Dinuba, and Reedley, moving between towns on train, on foot, and in the cars of friendly drivers. Then he headed for Fresno where, for a week, he divided his day-time hours between pool rooms, the jungles, and the depot. His road stake was being steadily whittled away by the cost of food and cheap lodgings. Job reports from jungle companions were vague and uncertain, with "Nothing doing" as the most common word on prospects for work. Finally, with a dollar and a half left in his pocket, he went to the employment agency he had visited several weeks before. There was still a posted notice about a construction job at Sand Creek. Two or three turbaned Hindoos were talking about this job to a man at a desk in the corner. "It's an easy job," he was telling them, "only eight hours a day and no Sunday work, because it's a county contract. Two and a quarter a day, fine working conditions, and Mr. Grey is a good boss. Stage goes out at five o'clock tomorrow morning." The Hindoos understood little of this, but it was made clear to them that the job cost them a dollar. "What about the stage fare?" asked Ben. "Three and a half, but you can pay that back whenever you are ready, after you have earned it." Ben paid his dollar, and was told to be on hand before five the next morning.

The stage, a rather ancient converted truck, was full when it pulled out the next morning. There were fifteen men bound for Sand Creek, about half being Hindoos, several Mexicans and Slavs, and two or three that Ben took to be Americans. A rocking, racking pull up the Sierra foothills brought them to Sand Creek at about seven-thirty. Four or five men were waiting to take the stage as it started back. The newcomers were shown a tent, given a hasty breakfast, and put to work at eight o'clock.

"Can you handle a fresno?" asked the foreman to whom Ben reported. Being told that he could not, the foreman told him to pick up a shovel, and assigned him to a group of seven men who were leveling dirt in a fill. Working with them was a man with a horse-drawn scraper—an instrument here known as a fresno, Ben gathered. This was one of four groups, making about thirty men in all, who were grading for an extension of the Sand Creek Road. It was tight, hard work—harder, Ben thought, than rustling orange boxes. For in the packing house the pace-setter had been the piece-rate system; here it was a driving, snarling foreman. There was no leaning on shovels, no talking, just unremitting hard work while hands blistered and back ached. Yet, Ben noticed, the crews were slovenly and inefficient. Some of the men were old, some were physical wrecks. The Hindoos, who made up about a third of the total work force, were clearly unskilled in handling picks and shovels. Four men were fired in the course of the morning, two because they were obviously unfitted for the work, one because he talked back to the foreman when he was cussed for being careless, and one who was ordered to "get his time" for no reason at all that Ben could see.

The noon break was welcome. With three or four others Ben sat on the grass outside the mess tent after eating. "That's the drivin'est foreman I ever worked under," said a youth who had come up with Ben. "Hell," said another, "Grey's going to pay a forfeit of fifteen dollars a day if he doesn't finish this stretch of road by July first. No wonder he's pushing." "He'd make more speed if he had better men," remarked a third. "What the Hell good are those rag-heads on a job of this sort. And the wine bums are worse." "From what I hear he'd lose more than his forfeit if he hired good men and kept them," replied the second speaker. "Figure it out for yourself. He's got thirty men on the job. If a man lasts two days here he's lucky. Grey gets a buck out of every stage fare, and half the blood money you paid to that gyp agency at Fresno. He's one of the bastards that makes his money from the three gang system—one gang working, one gang coming, one gang going." He turned to Ben. "How long do you think you'll last?" "I figure to build up a little stake," said Ben, "after I make enough to pay the fare." "You'll lose your job as soon as you have worked that fare off," was the pleasant promise from the other.

The afternoon was hot and dry. The motley crew struggled along under the burning sun and the lash of the foreman's tongue. Two threw down their shovels in disgust, and were fired. The working day ended with the men in a mood of sullen discontent. This discontent was heightened, for the newcomers, when they were shown their sleeping quarters. These were in an

open tent, about 20 feet by 50 feet in size. A third of the tent,
separated from the rest by a strand of rope and a board near the
floor, was used to stable six or eight horses. The work crew
occupied the rest of the tent. There was no floor. Blankets were
spread on a thin layer of dirty hay. Water was piped to a trough
outside the tent, but of other conveniences there were none.
When the foreman looked in, one of the men complained mildly
about being quartered in a stable. "Teamsters sleep with their
horses," was the reply. "You're no better than a teamster." The
night was chill, the ground was hard, and Ben's coverings were
far from adequate. From the twisting, turning, and coughing of
his fellow-sleepers he judged that others suffered in the same
way.

The morning stage brought a dozen more men from Fresno,
and three men boarded it for the return trip. Ben noticed three
or four others starting off on foot, with their blanket rolls on
their backs.

The second day repeated the story of the first. The sun beat
down on the exposed hillside on which they worked. The foreman cursed, men quit. Two men fought with swinging shovels,
and both were fired. Ben, who had aimed at a stake of fifteen or
twenty dollars, adjusted his sights. As soon as he had earned
enough to get back to the valley he would tell the foreman to
go to Hell. In mid-afternoon three men walked into camp and
asked the foreman for work. "Got all the men we can use," he
said. Ben spent another cold and restless night.

On the afternoon of the next day the handle of Ben's shovel,
which had been cracked when he got it, broke. "What a damn
fool you are," said the foreman. "I ought to charge you for
that. Go get your time." To Ben's "It was no good to begin
with" the foreman retorted "The Hell it wasn't, it was a new
shovel." "Well, you know what you can do with it now," said
Ben. Ben's time card showed that he had earned six dollars and a
quarter, and that he owed two and a quarter for board and
three-fifty for stage fare. He pocketed fifty cents as his earnings
for almost two days of work. Counting in his employment
agency fee, he had lost fifty cents on the undertaking. And he
was forty miles from the valley where he might find another job
or, at any rate, friendly jungles.

The driver of the scraper, who seemed to be a local man, told Ben that he might find work with Harris, contractor on the Tulare section of the Sand Creek Road. Ben shouldered his roll and started off on the five-mile climb to Harris' camp.[6]

The descriptions in Mills's novel of conditions at the road-building camp are very close to those he gave in his report to the Immigration Commission. In his report he added that when the work crew grew larger at Ball's camp (Grey's camp in the novel), some of the men were forced to sleep out in the open because there was no room in the tent. The practice of only giving work to men who arrived by stage was also emphasized in the report. When he arrived at the camp on foot Mills was refused work, yet three men who arrived later by stage were given jobs. The action in the novel also took place at a time when more work was available at the camp. When Mills arrived only one crew, with eight men, was at work, and the stage fare had been reduced from $3.50 to $3.00.

Mills concluded in his report that the issue of whether direct fraud could be proven or not was a minor matter compared to how the facts about Ball's camp threw light on the employment agency system in general: "Not only does the private organization of the employment agency system furnish a haphazard, accidental and inefficient method of connecting the man with the job, but it is an absurd one as well. Consider how paradoxical a system is that leaves the remedying of the conditions of uncertainty and casuality in our labor market in the hands of the very persons who profit by such conditions!"[7]

III

Private employment agencies and their deficiences received significant attention by Mills and by investigators at the Immigration Commission and the Industrial Relations Commission because of the belief at the time that unemployment was caused to a large degree by disorganization in labor markets. Mills and both commissions supported this viewpoint, which formed the basis for the commissions' strong recommendations for a system of publicly supported employment agencies.[8]

The California Immigration Commission made its case for state employment agencies in its December 1914 *Report on Unemploy-*

ment. The commission made several recommendations in the report for reducing unemployment, the first two being "the creation of a state bureau of labor exchanges" and "the enacting of more stringent laws for the regulation of private employment agencies." The commission argued, with extensive quotations from reports in other states, that current methods of obtaining job information were almost totally useless. Providing job information was as "legitimately a piece of public work as is the supplying of weather reports, crop statistics, soil surveys, knowledge of foreign markets, methods of cultivation, and the like." Mills made his case for public agencies in his report to the Immigration Commission on the Sand Creek Road situation, where he claimed that "a scientifically organized and intelligently conducted system of putting the man where he is wanted and where he will fit, would appear to be the *sine qua non* of any permanently satisfactory organization of labor and industry."[9]

A major reason for the emphasis at the time on public labor exchanges as a remedy for unemployment was that successful systems had been set up recently in Europe, most notably in England and Germany. The European attitude toward unemployment was seen by many U.S. reformers as more humane than the unregulated chaos of U.S. labor markets. This view dominated the conclusions of the U.S. Commission on Industrial Relations (CIR) as much as it did the findings of Mills and the California Immigration Commission. William Leiserson, in an CIR report on "The Labor Market and Unemployment," claimed that the "essence" of the unemployment problem was the irregularity of employment caused by "consistent dropping of employees from the pay rolls, because of seasonal fluctuations in demand or industrial depression, or unsystematic methods of hiring, grading and discharging employees." Leiserson argued a solution to the problem of irregular employment required the organization of "the labor market on a systematic business-like and efficient basis. . . . This is generally recognized as the first step in any intelligent attempt to deal with the problem."[10]

Reports emphasizing public employment agencies as a central weapon in the attack on unemployment acknowledged that employment agencies did not provide a final solution to the problem. Leiserson, for example, made a point of noting that public agencies could not find workers jobs that did not exist. Mills also saw limitations in the agencies. After his hobo travels were over, he voiced his doubts about the usefulness of a system of public employment agencies in dealing with the unemployment problems of itinerant workers:[11]

> The ultimate reorganization and coordination of the employment agency systems that is to be hoped for will remedy to some considerable extent the evils of unemployment that go hand in hand with the present system and with the present organization of industry. But our observations lead us to believe that in too many cases the fundamental reasons are other than mere maladjustment, lying rather in the nature of the work open to these men. . . . The weary monotony, the emptiness, the at times agonizing harshness of such kinds of rough occasional labor as will be offered them under this or any other system, will be unrelieved. Even if the system works perfectly, it will mean nothing but an endless succession of such jobs. The protracted jag, the period of bumming between such jobs, are in part due to a desire for relief from and a reaction to these wearisome periods of work. These conditions and phases of the unemployment problem that no mere organization of the labor market can relieve cannot be ignored.[12]

Mills's concerns about the effectiveness of a system of national labor exchanges add to Leiserson's observation that labor exchanges could not place workers in jobs that did not exist. Mills saw in addition that labor exchanges could not place workers in jobs they were not qualified for or did not want, an observation drawn from his lumber industry report, in which he concluded that itinerant workers essentially were trapped in a cycle of secondary, temporary jobs. He stated this conclusion forcefully in a passage in his journal:

Sacramento, June 24, 1:30 P.M.
     A life easy to drift into, this, very easy, but hard to drift out of. In fact one can't drift out of it; you've got to take yourself by the blooming nape of your neck and pull yourself out of it. And to few is given the power to do this.
     This is the normal system by which an astoundingly large percentage of all our manual labor is done. It is not at all abnormal, but the normal method of living that hundreds of thousands, yea millions, must look forward to all their working lives. There is no way out for the most of them.

Mills also found that many of the men in the seasonal or casual cycle were accustomed to their life and did not want it to change. Organized public labor exchanges would "afford a way out of casuality for those who are still in the stage at which they have the desire and the initiative to escape," but he concluded that most casuals were not of this type:

> Observations, returns for "life-histories" of casuals, indicate the great extent to which the class of seasonal laborers is made up of drifting, non-resisting casuals. Seventy per cent of the men questioned by our agents had no future plans and evidently no desire to escape from the life of a "floater.". . . The proportion of the migratory casuals I have met who fall into the class [of those who do not have the initiative to escape] is strikingly large, so large that to neglect them, to entirely emphasize the other element comes close to being a gross mis-statement of the problem and of conditions as they are.[13]

Mills's analysis is an important one. He had a deeper understanding of the realities of labor markets than did those who saw labor exchanges as a panacea for the contemporary unemployment problem. His insight on this point, however, did not come from a better intuitive feeling for the working of the economy. Rather, it was based on what he saw and heard in his personal contacts with itinerants. In this respect, Mills's conclusions are a striking illustration of the importance of thoroughly understanding a problem in creating public policy.

5

Walking the Roads

THE RITUAL OF THE ROAD

Have you ridden the guts of the rattler,
Face pelted with burning sand?
Have the shacks kicked you off in the darkness,
Ditched in a horstile land?

Have you flopped in barns and in hay-stacks,
And on side-door Pullman floors?
Have you jungled in dirty hollows?
Have you dined on the bounty of whores?

Have you thrown your feet for a hand-out,
Weary, covered with dust,
Selling your soul for the scoffings,
Begging in vain for a crust?

Have you buried the name you were born with?
Is the line of your fathers dead?
Is a moniker all that is left you
To be scrawled on that last pauper's bed?

Why, then, you're a tried, sworn brother
Of the blithesome hobo crew——
You're one of the wrecks of Creation
Who drink of the Devil's brew,

You're one of earth's twisted vessels,
You're a loathsome "son of a toad"——
You're a carefree, joyous fellow
Of the Brotherhood of the Road.

I

Frederick Mills wrote these verses after his hobo journey was over.[1] The vocabulary included terms he heard and used while on the road (rattler = train; shack = railroad guard; horstile = hostile; flopped = slept; throw your feet = beg; side-door Pullman = boxcar; jungle = hobo gathering place; scoffings = food to add to jungle stewpot; moniker = nickname). Some of the experiences in the verses were his own (being kicked off trains by railroad guards in the dark, flopping in haystacks, using a false name). The others he heard about in jungle conversations. All were part of the life he experienced as he traveled the roads and rode the rails of the Central Valley. During these travels, he lived in a world that was different from any he had known before. With a distinct code of conduct, its own language, and its own traditions, this world stimulated Mills, and, besides composing verse, he wrote a great deal in his journal about his reactions.

Mills's observations of life on the road are consistent with other accounts of his time. John J. McCook's photos of hoboes stealing rides on trains, for example, illustrate several of the methods Mills used to travel in the Central Valley. Jack London's account of his adventures on the road used the same language, described the same techniques of travel, and discussed the same rules of daily life. The parallels between Mills's reactions to hobo life and those of Walter Wyckoff are particularly striking. Wyckoff was a new college graduate like Mills when he decided to work his way across the United States as a common laborer. His reactions to the sore muscles created by hard physical work after a life of study were the same as Mills's in Drake's packinghouse; his comments about the lack of an intellectual life in a Pennsylvania lumber camp were much like Mills's at Hume; and his description of a meal at a New England lodging house, where the table was covered by flies, was reminiscent of Mills's story about dinner at Dad's Hotel in Lindsay. Although Mills's observations were not unique, the purpose of his trip was different from that of most other observers. His motivation was not that of a storyteller or social critic, but one of an investigator who needed to make careful notes of itinerant life for use in developing public policy.[2]

Mills's writings about his travels tell about a way of life that has almost disappeared in the United States. Personal accounts of recent hobo journeys by Michael Mathers and Douglas Harper, for example, are about a different life than the one Mills saw. The itinerant working class reached its largest size and played its most important role in the economy between the Civil War and World War I. Technological and social changes beginning in the 1920s reduced the employment opportunities tramping workers needed in order to live. The 1930s saw a resurgence of itinerant life, but this was of a different kind— the 1930s migrants were refugees rather than true hoboes. Today, according to Harper, the last significant economic niche supporting a classic hobo life is the fruit harvest of the Pacific Northwest.[3]

Even in the few restricted areas where hobo life has survived, it is different from that of Mills's day. Much of the vocabulary is the same, as is the pattern of companionship Mills described, but many of the old rules of life on the road are gone. Mills was fascinated, for example, by the rules for keeping jungles liveable. In contrast, Mathers found surviving jungles a mess and jungle life essentially stamped out, especially on the East Coast. Recent accounts also find that the derelict proportion of the hobo population is much greater than before. Mills met many "unemployables," as he called these men, but not nearly in the numbers that exist today.[4]

II

The hobo jungle was the center of itinerant life in Mills's day. In visits to hobo camps throughout the Central Valley, he found the jungle to be more than a haphazard gathering place. It was a well-developed institution, with its own rules and patterns of life. In his journal he wrote a detailed description of jungles in early twentieth-century California:

Marysville, July 17, 1914

One of the most peculiar and distinctive features of the life of the itinerant is the jungle. In any railroad town of any size one will find jungles. Perhaps they are under a trestle near the station; perhaps they are by the side of a river or stream at the other side of the town. Wherever water is available and wood is handy jungles can exist, provided always that there is no molestation by horstile town or railroad bulls.

Here the ever-changing, ever-moving army of migratory workers and migratory non-workers—itinerants of every class, cook up their mulligans and their java. The ingredients of a jungle feed are scoffed up in many ways. The butcher and baker are appealed to, for a hand-out if possible, or at least to give enormous quantities of their goods for a small amount of money. Potatoes and onions are ravaged from nearby gardens. If a stray chicken wanders in the vicinity the richness of the stew is likely to be enhanced. . . . Java is usually carried along in small sacks. The trifling fact that it may have been used three or four times previously merely necessitates a little longer boiling.

The implements of war—the pots, pans, kettles, etc., are a fixed and stationary part of the jungle. They consist of lard cans, pails, perhaps now and then a real pan or kettle, with patched bottom and sides. The drinking cups are of similar manufacture, but smaller, bean cans, etc., often still with their rough and ragged edges at the top, being used. Forks and spoons are seldom present; knives are represented by an occasional pocket knife. Food is usually conveyed to the mouth by means of the fingers or by the use of small bits of wood. A table is a luxury. The ever-essential "boiling-up" can must not be forgotten—a large coal-oil can or drum, used to remove debris of vegetable, mineral, or animal origin from shirts and other clothes of all sorts.

All these pots, cups, etc., are parts of the jungle. To remove or destroy them, to appropriate them for continued individual use is a violation of the code of hobo ethics. You come, you use them, you go, leaving them in as good shape as you found them.

A shifting stream of life flows thru these jungles. . . . On one day there may be 20 men of all ages, colors, and nationalities (usually very few or no Greeks, Italians, and southern Europeans generally), cooking and boiling up, sleeping. The next day there may be 20 still there, yet every face may be different. Even on the same day different faces are seen at different hours in a large jungle. Enough for a jungle feed is scoffed up, cooked up, and eaten. Then the men go back up town. . . .

There is usually a hearty camaraderie in these jungles. If you have nothing to eat you are usually hailed and asked to join some group. This is not always the case, but usually there is some brother of the road willing to share his scoffings with a hungry fellow. . . .

The Marysville jungles are among the largest in the interior cities of California. Here where two railroad lines cross, the cross-roads of North, East, and West, a shifting, migratory army is in constant procession. The jungles lie between the Western Pacific tracks and the Feather River. They adjoin the city's dumping ground, 2–3 acres covered with refuse of every kind.

The jungles themselves are dirty. There are ten fire-places, and four or five fires are usually going at every hour of the day, with 15–20 men constantly here. The dumping grounds supply an unlimited number of tin cans, as well as a considerable amount of food for certain of the men. Two unique houses have been built from this refuse, which grace and distinguish these Marysville jungles. I counted the following materials used in their construction:

Great tin slabs, buckets, oil cans, lard pails, barrels, rubber-hose, rubber-coats, broken brooms and shovels, logs of wood, pots, kettles, old clothes, carpets, matting, oil cloth, bottles.

The door of one of these huts, made of tin, is locked, and has an auto number on it, while a small flag floats from a tin can over it. Enough ingenuity was shown in the construction of this one cabin to build a sky-scraper, if properly applied.

These jungles, moreover, have a large fly-catcher in the middle of the jungle area, so it is quite a stylish place. That fly-catcher, we trust, is young and ambitious. Digging the Panama canal with a shovel would be a mere child's job compared with the task that has been assigned to it.

After his hobo trip was over, Mills expanded upon his journal observations in a short paper about jungle life. He called the jungle "the unsung center of hobo life, its kitchen, bed room, bath room, its public forum, library, and bureau of information." The central role of jungles and the accepted rules of conduct suggested to Mills that itinerant life had a structure that migrants could count on as a source of refuge and comfort (rough as it was) in the same way that those in other walks of life could count on their home, their job, their family, or their church.[5]

Mills spent a good deal of time in various jungles sitting back and talking with fellow travelers. The stories he heard and the men he met made a strong impression:

Marysville, July 17, 1914

The life that one comes in contact with in these jungles is in many ways dwarfed, narrow, perverted, never having come to a full awakening and consciousness of its inherent value. But in many other ways this is atoned for. It has the strong, virile, pulsing beat of reality. Vulgar it is, and coarse, deprived of the joys of the higher life. But still is there a grip and a force to it, and to the men who live it. Tragedy they have seen, and felt, and know, and misery. And they have lived in a large world. They have seen life in many garbs and death in many disguises in the ends of all the earth. Perhaps it is a soldier, who pursued the fleeting Aquinaldo thru treacherous fever-ridden swamps in a land of wily natives. Or he may have braved the shots of Santiago and of San Juan. Many, many such are on the road. Perhaps it is an English cockney with his East End words and jokes. Or a sailor who has ploughed the seven seas (Bye many a tempest hadde his bearde been shacke) with tales of coral isles, of icy Alaskan waters, Raratonga and Kamchatka, Ceylon and Molekai [sic] dropping richly from his lips in the same breath. Perhaps it is a fake beggar, working a "sap," speaking six languages, with a training for the Catholic priesthood lying lightly on his shoulders. Or a "yegg," who has pulled off taps from Florida to Vancouver Island, mentioning incidentally jails he has served in, and bulls he has met. All these have I met and seen, and many others.

And the tales they tell are redolent of action, of life, tho life on the under-side of the shield, to be sure. Tales of icy lands, largely, of sunny climes, of wild places. . . . And ever thru them all, a red and bitter poison, echoes the passionate pulse of lust. They have tasted of them all, the warm, full-breasted women of the South Seas, the icy vampires of great cities, the loathsome creatures of Oriental tenderloins. . . . (Oh, it's sweet to hear the tales the troopers tell.) Ruined by it, "shot to pieces," in their own phrase, can a just god blame them? Denied more completely than if there were a Caesarian degree [sic] against it a monogamic life, rigid economic necessity has closed to them all thoughts of a normal home life.

Mills's comments about the "reality" and "grip" of the stories told by men he met suggest that he was not immune to the attractions of a life on the road. The daily adventure of getting by, the tales shared while sitting around jungles, the freedom to wander where and when one wanted, the new places seen today and to be seen tomorrow, all had an appeal that could not be denied.

III

Mills's travels along the hobo routes of the Central Valley had two distinct phases. The first came between his jobs in the orange and lumber industries as he traveled between Lindsay and Hume. The second came after his investigation of the Sand Creek Road crew when he left the San Joaquin Valley for the area north of Sacramento. In his journey between Lindsay and Hume, he traveled alone and walked or hitchhiked. He stopped at hobo centers in towns along the way to talk with other itinerants but did not spend much time in jungles. He was in the initial stage of hobo life, in which newcomers were called "road-kids" or "gay-cats." (Mills used the terms interchangeably. Jack London said there was an age distinction, "gay-cats" being older.) A hobo in this stage had little knowledge of the institutions and patterns of life on the road. Despite Mills's disguise, he traveled in this portion of his trip more like a college boy roughing it than as an experienced hobo.[6]

Mills's journal entries from this first phase of his journey provide a detailed account of daily life for the neophyte itinerant. Since the experiences he was having were new to him, he wrote about them at length. His account starts when he left Lindsay and ends when he arrived at Hume five days later:

Tulare—May 30, 1914—8 A.M.
    Walked for an hour and a half in the moonlight toward Tulare. The evening was cool and very pleasant, with a crescent moon in the sky and the stars like torches. An occasional auto shot by me as I plodded along. About three miles from Lindsay the orange groves came to an end, being succeeded by hay land, chiefly. Got a drink at a farmhouse windmill. Slept very com-

fortably in back of a large hay stack near the road. Got up at 6 A.M. Got my first hand-out at a small farm-house. Asked a sad-faced woman who came to the door for work to do for break-fast. She said that there was no work, but that I could have something to eat. She told me her son was bathing in the kitchen preparatory to going to Fresno, so that I would have to eat outside. The son was losing his eyesight and one more attempt to save it was to be made in Fresno that day. The agony of life it seems can't be left behind. We come across it at every turn of the road. In spite of my requests for work to do she would give me none. Handed me out package containing eggs and biscuits.

After starting off again I was overtaken by a young man driv-ing a large hay rake who had followed me half a mile, having seen me pass. He wanted to know if I was looking for work. Seeing nothing to be gained thru a job on a small ranch I was forced to refuse. He thanked me politely and turned back. . . .

Was picked up by a young mechanic in a machine and carried about ten miles to Tulare. It is impossible to hobo in peace thru this country. Willy-nilly one is picked up and carried along by kind-souled auto-owners. The country just swarms with machines.

Visalia—May 31, 1914—8:30 A.M.
Spent all day yesterday in Tulare R.R. station preparing [orange industry] report. . . . Ate supper in a Chinese restau-rant. . . .

Started out for Visalia at 7 P.M., since there was no group work of the kind I wanted [in Tulare]. The walking was very pleasant, so I kept on till about 9 o'clock. There were numerous irrigation ditches and small streams flowing over the almost absolutely level valley floor. Many machines kept shooting past in the night. Before turning in I took a bath at a wayside irriga-tion ditch. Felt like a god when I had sluiced some of the dirt off my back. A group passing in a machine laughed uproari-ously, but phased [sic] me not a whit. Flopped under an oak tree in a field, by the road, with enough hay under me to relieve the hardness of the ground. Got up at 6:30 on a cloudy morning. Struck at the first farmhouse for work for breakfast but was

sharply told there was none. The way of the "Tramp Royal" is
not always easy.

Was passed by a machine with a vacant seat beside the well-
dressed driver and felt mildly insulted after my previous experiences because I was not given a lift. However, a young farmer
soon came by in a cart and invited me to ride with him, apolo-
gizing because he had no auto to offer me. We talked about
work and general laboring conditions. . . .

Jogged all the way to Visalia getting in at about 8 o'clock. . . .
Ate a good breakfast at a little coffee joint run by two boys.

Dinuba—May 31—5:30 P.M.

Left Visalia about 9 A.M. Walked slowly out thru the residence district. Three spinsterly looking elderly ladies seated on
the porch of a house I passed watched me with expressions of
agonized pity. —"So young and so depraved." With pack on
back and a battered hat on my head I guess that I looked like a
lost soul to them.

Struck the main road running North and followed it for 4 or
5 miles thru alfalfa land with patches of haying land here and
there. Watered by many streams and ditches it seemed to be
ideal dairying country, as it is. Crossed a small river that looked
invitingly cool, but as the road was well travelled I hesitated to
jump in. Many machines were passing but none of the drivers
seemed as generous as the ones I had met before. Finally a
pleasant-spoken young chap picked me up and carried me about
five miles. He remarked that I looked young for the life I was
leading. . . .

Entered Dinuba at about 3 o'clock on a quiet Sunday afternoon, hot as blazes. People resting on the lawns and porches
looked queerly after me. I hit for the R.R. tracks and sat for 2
hours with two very interesting fellow travelers, in the shade of
a large water tank. . . .

I found a place where I could get a good meal and one quart
of ice water for 25 cents. Wrote up a few notes in a field by the
R.R. track while a bunch of kids were disporting themselves in a
pool near by. I think I will do the same a little later.

Sanger—June 1—10:30 A.M.

About 7:30 last night after the kids had finished their swimming I hit their swimming hole and ducked around for about five minutes. It certainly did feel like heaven. Walked about a mile out of Dinuba and flopped near the R.R. tracks in a small hay pile. With the moon shining full in my face, the night very sultry, and bothered by mosquitoes, I spent a rather uncomfortable night. The mosquito patrol was working to perfection, the sentry on duty sending out a hurry call for the reserves every time I disclosed a square inch of my body. And a most efficient reserve corps they were, too.

Got up about 6 and tramped into Reedley for breakfast. Passed a jungle just outside of town, but receiving no word of welcome hesitated to join them. Ate a prodigious breakfast in a Chinese restaurant in Reedley, consuming endless glasses of ice water. Talked for a few minutes with a "blanket stiff" who had come up from Visalia. Said there was no work yet, but [apri]cots would soon be ripe. . . . Left Reedley at 8:30 A.M. Hit the main road for Fresno shortly and followed it for about half an hour. Was then picked up by a young well-digger in a machine and carried clear to Sanger. The country between was very rich looking. Hay fields, alfalfa land, peach and apricot orchards, vineyards abound. Watered by numerous irrigation ditches. Crossed King's River—a large fast-flowing stream—just out of Reedley. Crops were all said to be very rich this year. Reached Sanger 10 A.M. . . .

Am making good time across the country, left Tulare, approximately 50 miles away, late Saturday night. Here in Sanger early Monday morning.

Minkler—June 3, 1914

Am on my way to Hume—at Minkler, a little station on the Santa Fe about 8 miles east of Sanger, lying close up to the foothills.

Monday night . . . I got my roll from the chop-house and slept under some trees about one half-mile from town. Had a rather hard bed but at least was not troubled by mosquitoes.

Tuesday morning while waiting for instructions for which I had written, I strolled out along the Hume road. Climbed up to the flume from Hume and watched the great planks come shooting down from their sixty-mile ride. Lay under a tree for three hours—my first real relaxation since leaving home. Being merely underneath the bough, even without the other essentials of the old Tent-makers paradise was sufficient for me after the strenuous period I had spent. Lunched on six oranges I stole from the wagon of a passing Jap. The virus of the life must be getting into my veins, as I felt absolutely no compunctions. Strolled back to town and got my mail— Then went out to a small stream and rested and read for another couple of hours. . . .

[I met] a likeable young chap—about 24—rather well educated, having gone to school, he said, for ten years. We struck up quite an acquaintance and after we had eaten in a Chinese Noodle joint, from which I pilfered a sign reading, "No Bad Talk Allowed Here," we found a barn with an abundant supply of hay, I gave him one of my blankets, and we turned in. . . .

In the morning we talked of "jungling up," but as he had $1.15 and I had $1.65 we felt rich and bought a breakfast at 25 cents each. . . .

I shipped my roll to Hume for 25 cents and set out, heart free and legs loose, swinging along with two days of wonderful mountain walking in front of me after the wearisomely flat and monotonous valley floor. Picked up a ride shortly after starting, which benefited me very little, for it carried me a mile off the right road before I knew it. The correct road lay but a short stretch across country to the South, but a slough of evil omen lay between. I made an attempt to wade across and save two miles, but I found the soft mud a little too treacherous.

Once on the right road I swung out again and soon caught up with a dark-featured Mexican going the same way. We exchanged greetings and I tried to strike up a conversation, but found that he knew practically no English. With the aid of what Spanish I knew, however, we had quite an agreeable walk of several miles. He was going to Tokay, near Reedley, he said, where his "trabajo" was on a railway line. By working my little Spanish overtime I managed to get a good deal of information about his class and the work they do. . . .

Reached Minkler at 12:20. Had a good lunch. Wrote up notes in Santa Fe station at Minkler till 2:40.

Dunlap—June 4—8 A.M.

Left Minkler at 2:40 yesterday. Road along level stretch of country for some miles, then rising slowly. Then passed thru a pretty little valley—Citrus Cove—Hay, and a few orange trees being planted. From there rose gradually—stunted oaks—passed through low hills—rocky, barren. Trees became thicker and walking more pleasant. Road wound through ravines and along hillsides. Ever behind me about two hundred yards a team and wagon. I swung on waiting for it to catch up to me so that I might get a lift, but, like Tantalus, I was doomed to have it never reach me. When the road became a little steeper I left it altogether behind.

Reached Squaw Valley at 6:15. Made a meal from a can of pineapple and a few crackers. Was told that work was scarce at Hume. . . .

Walked on from Squaw Valley to Dunlap after supper. 10 miles. Moon was almost full; lit up country, which was beautiful in the moonlight. "If you would visit fair Melrose aright, Go visit it by the pale moonlight." Great shadows lay across the road which wound thru valleys and around hills. . . .

I continued on, reaching Dunlap at 10 P.M. Opened a barn door and crawled in—had no blankets—there was but a little hay in the place, but I found a large horse-blanket which kept me fairly warm. Spent a fitful night. Up at 6:30. Breakfast at hotel. Am off now for Dunlap cut-off, which saves some three or four miles. Came 29 miles yesterday. Between 15 and 20 more to go.

Hume, June 4th, 6 P.M.

Left Dunlap at 8:30 and struck out for trail I had been told of. Had a little trouble finding the right trail, but was directed to it by several Indian families living in the hills back of Dunlap.

From here, Mills's journal begins the account of his work at the Hume lumber camp. The sleeping places, the people, the handouts at farmhouses, the cheap restaurant meals, and the techniques of travel he wrote about on the way from Lindsay to Hume were typical experiences of thousands of "road-kids" like Mills.

IV

In his initial period of hoboing, Mills also met many of the types of men he was to live with in the following weeks. Since these were his first close contacts with men on the road, he spent considerable time writing about his impressions in his journal and later, in more detail, in a report he wrote for the Immigration Commission entitled "Scenes and Incidents 'On the Road.' " The descriptions in this report are among the most detailed Mills gave of his encounters with individual itinerants. He attempted in these sketches to depict "the general character of the men studied and their attitude toward certain things, in a way that mere statistical data cannot do." He labeled the encounters according to the location where they occurred:[7]

A Tank at Dinuba
On a hot, quiet Sunday afternoon, while the townspeople, in light summer clothes, aired themselves on lawns and beneath trees, we sat beneath a water tank near the railroad track, that lodestone that draws, as a magnet does, all the shiftless breed in whose veins the germs of wanderlust are rife. Of my two companions, one was a man well over middle age, white-haired, white-whiskered and red-faced, with fat pursy cheeks hanging from his jaws in heavy jowls like those of a great Dane. Rather short and stout, he carried his heavy pack with the aid of a light cane. (It is the exception, it may be noted, to find a man of this age on the road, tho there are some; the average tramp or casual worker has become a fixed "city bum" or has left the road in some way, before he is far beyond middle age.) The other, about thirty years old, was tall and muscular, face lean and clean-shaven, tanned to the color of old leather. The lines on his face, not those of weakness and dissipation that characterize many of the type, rather betokened him as one who took his living from society instead of trusting to society's charity for it.
The conversation at such chance meetings is concerned largely with prospects for work and general conditions in this regard in

the various regions from which the different men have come. Ostensibly all members of this migratory class are looking for employment. The pass-word of hobo-land, exchanged wherever hoboes meet, is, "Well, what's doing?"

The old man, called "Dad" by the other, had just come up from Lindsay, where he had been picking oranges. Cheated by fellow-workmen, imposed on by eating-houses, persecuted by owners and growers, he had left, and damned them most eloquently in all-inclusive phraseology. He branded as a false-hood, with many qualifying, tho unprintable epithets, the statements that men had been needed at Lindsay, saying that there were men out of work all the time.

The increasing number of Japanese workers who were said to be completely driving out American labor, was discussed. In one mood the Japanese were cursed inexorably, while a moment later, the lean pessimistic hobo remarked that he hoped the time was coming when they would own all the land in the country and every "damned American" would be driven out. . . .

The talk then turned to "bulls," that is sheriffs, constables, "fly-cops," marshals, and all the other minions of the law. "Dad" cursed one Court Smith, Marshal of Tulare, now a candidate for sheriff, one of whose portraits, on a political notice, stared us in the face, from a side of the tank. This "lean, hungry-looking ——— of a ———" as he was termed, was trying to prevent all sleeping in haystacks and boxcars, which, of course, violated all the fundamental principals [sic] of the Magna Charta of hobo-land. Tales of how he had maliciously broken up "jungles" by kicking over pots of stew and of coffee were told. "Dad" stated that the tramp vote would be cast solidly against him, but as the other "bo" quizzically remarked, "No one on the bum gets a vote anyway, so that won't hurt him." The present Sheriff of Tulare County was given the honor of being the only man or thing in Creation that the loquacious "Dad" did not curse. The omni-denunciatory old man, whose only pleasure seemed to be to launch virulent floods of abuse at every available object, stated that the present sheriff was "a perfect gentleman," which was doubtless the highest word in his meagre lexicon of praise.

We adjourned late in the afternoon, the lean and hungry Cassius heading north, while the pursy old curser of all things said he was going to stay round Dinuba that night.

These two, tho widely different in many ways, were both types of the itinerant vagabond, working as little as possible in order to live, taking no thought of the morrow. Tho neither was fundamentally vicious or criminal, the descent into criminality is an easy and inviting road ever open to men of this class.

A "Jungle" at Sanger

[At a jungle] near Sanger, one bright June day, there were perched on boxes and reclining on the ground, four hoboes. On the one side, from the country road, prosperous farmers looked scornfully at them. On the other, from passing train windows, lolling sons of Luxury shuddered a little at the thought of the wickedness in the group, and thanked their Lord that they were not of such as these.

The hobo group, tho they toiled not neither did they spin, were arrayed as Solomon in all his glory never was. In blue overalls, cast-off clothes of many kinds, unshaven and for the most part unwashed, yet was the joy of life keen within them as they sat in the sun and talked of many things. Two of them were "on the yegg"—that is, they were criminal hoboes waiting for a chance to pull off a "tap," anything from robbing a defenseless woman to blowing up a bank safe. These two were of the more intelligent hobo class, and tho, as I later ascertained, undoubtedly yeggs, were not at all viciously mean on the surface. Between 35 and 45 years old, they were much better dressed than the average tramp. Both wore typical blue overalls but had woolen trousers beneath them and were equipped with light, strong shoes. "Blackie," one of these, was of medium height and of wiry, tho not muscular build, being a trifle narrow-chested. With an intelligent oval face, brown eyes and a rather quizzical drawl when he spoke, he was far from being unprepossessing, tho having about a three day's growth of beard on his face. The other was also of medium height but of heavier build, with a rather prominent stomach. His black hair was short, thin and streaked with grey, while a round face was decorated with a brown mustache. Below his jaw, his neck sloped off

in sleek, well-fed curves to his chest, as those of successful
bankers and brokers are apt to do. His opened shirt revealed on
his breast a tattooed heart with two clasped hands. The third
member of the party was a "road-kid" or "gay-cat" (myself),
while to the fourth I applied the name Tomlinson at first sight.
About 30 years old, weighing about 130 pounds, he was dressed
in a seedy grey suit, a checkered old cap, and a dirty grey shirt,
once white, with a string of a necktie. His hatchet face, with a
markedly retreating chin, was burned red to the color of brick-
dust, while his eyes were blearily moist and bloodshot, due to a
perpetual jag from which he was always recovering. His hands,
large for the size of his body, were covered with great freckles.
Tho raised in San Francisco, there never was a more typical
cockney seen in the East End of London. Tomlinson was a
"whiskey bum," a poor weak little victim of his thirst for drink.
At this time he was just recovering from a bad two day's [sic]
drunk, during which time he had lost his roll of blankets. Once
a lawyer's clerk in San Francisco, well fixed, with a good future,
the weak, soulless little thing in the shape of a man had
become, while still young, a useless, drifting derelict, veins hardened, ambition gone, fire burnt out. Surely "a viper lurketh in
ye wine cup red."

The talk, as we sat there thru the afternoon, covered a wide
range of subjects. Tomlinson did most of the talking, laying his
empty little soul bare before us, as he told of the things he had
done, the devilish life he had lived, the things he was capable of
doing. He cursed the fact that the "black ——— ———
———," meaning Mexicans, were driving men out of work.
Blackie drawled that when everybody had been driven out of
work, all would be "on the bum," which is evidently the millen-
ium [sic] of hobo dreams. It was stated that Mexicans and Japs
could get this work because white men would not keep a job for
more than a few days, only long enough to get the small
"stake" needed for a drunk. Tomlinson spoke of work in the
woods and Blackie remarked, "Damn working in the woods."
Then the loquacious cockney told of his prowess as a cement
worker, and "Blackie" took the opportunity to consign cement
working in general to the nethermost regions of Hell. As orange
picking, tree planting, haying, harvesting were mentioned in

"Blackie" cursed them all. He wanted no work he said, tho if a
nice easy job were brought to him he might take it. "Yes" said
his partner, "but it would have to be damned easy." The two
had been besought and begged to take a job that morning, but
had refused. With a quizzically humorous drawl "Blackie" told
of the task they were having dodging work. They were retreating northward as the crops ripened and help was wanted in the
south. . . .

The talk drifted to the market price of hay, then to the preva-
lence of the habit of mortgaging homes to buy autos. Tomlinson
said he had struck one man for a "hand-out" as he was fixing
his machine, and was told that there was no food in the house.
The corpulent hobo remarked that most automobile owners
were poorer than we were. Somebody mentioned bad times.
"Hell," said "Blackie," "these ain't bad times. Here I am lying
on a raisin box and don't have to work"—a piece of most sensi-
ble and philosophical reasoning.

The conversation was interrupted by the passage on the road
of an enormous "coon," a veritable whale of a man, staggering
under a roll of blankets apparently large enough for three men.
The color line would appear to have been drawn among the
Brethren of the Road, for we laughed at his ridiculous appearance and said nothing to him.

A flood of vulgar tenderloin talk almost unbelievably coarse
was started by some chance remark. They had all "taken their
fun where they'd found it, they had ranged and they'd rogued
in their time" and their tales were not sweet to hear. The multi-
farious experiences of "Blackie" and his pal included recollec-
tions of tenderloin habitués from coast to coast. In depths of
evil the loquacious Tomlinson could not even compare with the
less voluble thoroughbreds of the road. Poor weak little Tomlinson "with scarce the soul of a louse," he had neither the
strength of goodness nor of wickedness, tho indeed the roots of
sin were there.

There were represented here the two most widely different
types found on the road; the cringing, whining derelict, fawning
for a crust of bread on the one hand, and on the other the type,
usually strong and healthy, able to work but refusing to do so,
who do not ask for a livelihood but take it.

A Morning at a Railroad Station

At railway stations even more than at tanks, "jungles" or other places scattered along the railroad track, one is usually likely to find collections of casuals of all types. Not only do the regular hoboes, "blanket stiffs" and migratory workers who generally frequent the track gather here, but local "town bums" and unemployed of various types are to be found in these places. Such a collection I saw gather, pass along, and disperse one morning at Sanger.

The night before, the weariest looking mortal I had ever seen trudged haltingly up to me as I sat on the station platform. A young man of 24, he had just walked down from Hume, blistering his feet so in the course of the walk that he could hardly stand. He had worked there as a wood-buck for 2½ days at the hardest job, he swore, that mortal man ever devised or the Lord ever permitted. We struck up an acquaintance, slept together in a near-by barn and in the morning sat and talked by the station again. As a type of the young casual, his case was interesting. Raised in Chicago, he had ten years [sic] schooling and then had learned the trade of pressman in a newspaper office, at which he had worked for several years. Just one year before, prompted by a roving spirit, he had come out to California. All that summer he had worked in a Stone-Webster construction camp, getting $2.75 a day. When that was done, having quite a "stake," he had "bummed" it for several months till his money was gone. Since then he had worked at many things, holding various jobs for a few days till he had a couple of dollars, spending the time in between "on the bum." The previous winter, alone or with companions he would pick up for short intervals, he had "jungled" his way over almost the entire state. His ambition now was to gather a large enough "stake" to go back home to his family in style for the coming winter. The following summer he planned to come out again to California, finding a steady job at his trade, if possible. . . .

This boy had worked at Ball's Camp on the Sand Creek Road for two days and gave me my first information in regard to conditions there, stating that it was an employment agency game.

Young, intelligent, really attractive, this youth represents the best type found on the road. Neither vicious nor lazy, they start the life merely prompted by a youthful spirit of wanderlust. But inevitably, if they stay with it, the life gets into their blood. One of the most pitiful tragedies of the road is the transformation of such a youth into a shiftless, inefficient casual laborer.

As we sat at the station the life of the road passed by us and around us. Two mature looking men with weather-beaten faces, walked in from Fresno with clean white packs and stout clothes, not "bums" but seriously after work. They took a freight as it passed, headed for Porterville where they had heard of a power-house job.

Next a group of four arrived from Fresno, a seedy, disreputable lot, of the "wine-bum" type. First came one of them with a liquor-reddened face and a robust-appearing frame which was belied by the evident internal weakness of the man. He spoke with a thick burr in his voice that betokened his Scotch ancestry. He had no blankets, having left Fresno while drunk, he said. His three mates slouched up, one a plain tattered "bum" and one with an inauspiciously drooping eyelid that gave him the appearance of constantly winking as it screwed up one side of his face. The third bore the evident signs of being a hard drinker—a very red face with a straggly mustache, a nose bloated at the end into a red ball, and round, poppy, blood-shot red eyes. All appeared to be men in the neighborhood of forty years of age. They asked of the possibility of work, and talked of the jobs they had had. The poppy-eyed one told of a fine job, knocking rust off a pipe line, that he "shouldn't have give up." They also passed the word of a local freight out of Fresno which had a socialist crew who would "ditch" nobody. Thus are such news items passed from mouth to mouth in hobo-land. All these men, tho none of them old in years, were aged, decrepit, and fit for the ash-barrel as far as productive utility was concerned. Burnt out and dead, they belonged strictly to the "unemployable" class. . . .

"Blackie" and his partner and the little cockney were sitting in a group apart, as the rest of us sat near the depot platform. A motley collection we made, "Bums," "Boes," "Blanket-stiffs" of various kinds. Ten of us at 9 o'clock on a bright June morning, with the country just awakening to the busy throb of a new day. And there was no place for us. We were the extra cogs, the useless parts in the great industrial machine.

Apparently Mills did not consider these descriptions of his encounters with itinerants important. When asked by the National Archives in 1955 to supply copies of his Immigration Commission reports for their files, he sent all his reports except the one on "Scenes and Incidents." Perhaps he believed the report did not add anything of interest to knowledge about itinerant life. If so, he was mistaken. These accounts provide a detailed sample of the personalities, lifestyles, and conversations one could expect to experience on a trip "hoboing" it across the Central Valley in his time. Several features of hobo life stand out in these descriptions. Knowledge of current events and trends was widespread. Discussion topics ranged from the willingness of Japanese and Mexican workers to stay on a job while "American" itinerants moved on to the practice of people mortgaging their houses to buy automobiles. A distinctive attitude toward the law is evident—most sheriffs and marshals were cursed, and yeggs (criminals) among the hobo population were accepted as part of the daily scene. Central traditions of hobo life are discussed—everyone is ostensibly looking for work and jobs are the common topic in every group. The distinctive "types" among the constantly shifting population are identified, from men eager for work to wine-bum unemployables, road-kids new to the road, and yeggs looking for a "tap." Together these descriptions counter the stereotyped image of itinerants as a homogeneous group of lazy, shiftless men. In reading them, one can better understand what it meant to be a member of the groups sitting in the sun beside the tracks while the "sons of Luxury" rode "on the cushions" and gazed from passing trains.[8]

6

Riding the Rails

Stockton, June 22, 10 A.M.

It was 12:30 [A.M.] and dark; the ground was rough and uneven; there were several men, not particular in regard to their methods, trying to prevent us from boarding her. If one attempts to board her as she slowly starts, he is sure to get "ditched," as a shack or bull will pitch him off. He must wait until she is well under way, outside the yards if possible.

As she reached the crossing, gathering speed all the time, many dark forms disentangled themselves from the thousand night-shadows, and the hobo army attempted to board her. With a gang of this size, the train going fast, the shacks and bulls can keep only part of them off. There is the sharp run as the car that you want to board approaches you, the reach for the handle, and the leap in the dark for where you know the step should be; and if you strike it you are on. One of the group that we were waiting with failed to make her, and there were doubtless others. Those who wait far out usually make her if they can board her at the speed she has then attained. Once you are on her you climb to the top and look for a place to get out of the wind. You may have to ride between cars, hanging onto the iron handles all night, with the biting wind chilling your every nerve, inviting the loosening of the fingers or the false step that means death. Or you may have to sit out on the top with the wind of a 30 or 40 mile an hour train trying to blow the clothes off your body. No hobo resorts to the rods at night, and only when necessary during the day. If the gods are extremely propitious you may find an open box car, but usually the regular freights for long hauls (the "manifests") carry only loaded cars.

I

This passage from Mills's journal describes his first experience "riding the rails." During the month he spent crisscrossing the Central Valley after his work on the road construction crew, he learned much about the ways of hobo life. By the end of these weeks of nearly constant movement, he had graduated from the status of a "road-kid" to that of a seasoned itinerant. Mills became a member of the vast army hopping freights described by Jack London in his reminiscences of his days on the road.[1]

The railroad was a central feature of itinerant life. Almost invariably jungles were located near rail lines because the life they represented was a creation of the railroad and dependent upon it. There were several ways to ride a train. Before his hobo days, Mills had experienced only one—riding "on the cushions," that is, inside as a paying passenger. By the time his itinerant travels were over, he had a much broader vision of the possibilities of train travel. His preferred way of traveling during his hobo journey was blind baggage, or on the blind. This was on the front platform of a baggage car or mailcar. The blind was relatively comfortable, although conspicuous and thus subject to discovery. He also rode at times on the deck (on top of the train), in a reefer (refrigerator car), in a side-door Pullman (boxcar), and hanging from the iron steps on the side of a car. When he was most adventurous, he tried riding the blades (between the bouncing, flashing wheels of a passenger car), the bumpers (which all cars of the time had in order to cushion the impact of car against car), and the rods (also beneath cars, like riding the blades). About the only method he did not try was riding the cowcatcher (presumably to avoid the direct exposure to dust and insects at forty miles per hour).

As Mills learned, catching and riding trains was a dangerous business that required great skill. In 1908 the Interstate Commerce Commission estimated that over 47,000 men had been killed in the preceding decade attempting to ride trains illegally. Moreover, shacks and bulls at times were not gentle in their treatment of hoboes, and one had to know how to avoid them and how to deal with the threat they represented. It did not take long for Mills to come to appreciate the knowledge required to steal rides successfully on the railroads.[2]

Although most people in Mills's time had seen a freight train passing by loaded with hoboes, his accounts of his train trips provided

A typical "jungle" scene. The "java" was probably made from used coffee grounds scavenged from the trash. Library of Congress.

Riding on the rods, "Providence Bob" and "Philadelphia Shorty" on their "tickets," 1894. The Butler-McCook Homestead Collection, courtesy of the Antiquarian and Landmarks Society, Inc., Hartford, Connecticut.

details of what it actually meant to ride as a hobo. Mills's record of his freight-hopping days is also notable for its tales about hobo train travel. Train stories—ranging from humorous to gruesome—were a common topic in every jungle. They were a part of the tradition of the road and were daily fare in the existence of almost every hobo.

II

Mills wrote several descriptions of trips he took by train. His first account is about a trip from his job on the Sand Creek Road to Stockton. He started this journey by walking to Selma, where he joined a group of itinerants waiting to catch a freight to Fresno and Stockton. Since this was the first of his railroad experiences, he wrote at length about the journey:

Stockton, June 22, 10 A.M.

I had shipped my blanket to Stockton, so as to be free to travel by freight. I ate supper in, not the typical Chink restaurant, but a Japanese one, where a course (also coarse) meal cost 20 cents.

About 8 o'clock the freight took the siding to let several passengers go by. As she pulled out we waited for her down the track, and all boarded a side-door Pullman with the door knocked out. Within there was a single tall, lean hobo, who maintained a sphynx-like [sic] silence the whole time.

We tore along in the darkness, and lying head out of the open door in the rush of wind, I tried to compose a bit of hobo doggerel that was running in my mind.

We pulled into Fresno a little before ten, and as soon as the freight had slowed up we jumped out and tore out of the yards. The R.R. yards here extend for a long distance on each side of the station, and are closely patrolled by the railroad cops, who give short shrift to tramps and hobos, and other gentry of the road. We walked a mile or so to the other end of town, where at a crossing near the yard limits we waited for the regular northbound freight to be made up. We saw several other weary knights of the road lying here also, as this is the regular station on a regular route north-bound for hobos.

Dozing and napping in the rather cold evening air we spent several hours waiting. The train made innumerable false starts in switching before she finally pulled out.

When she finally "Highballed" and started out, there was a shack with a lantern near the front, several railroad bulls along the sides, and a shack at the end of her. . . .

This night I found a place of refuge a few minutes after I climbed to the top of her. I lay down by another benighted traveler to avoid some of the wind. Soon a form loomed up, staggering weirdly along the top and yelled thru the roar of the train that there was an empty "reefer" a few cars back. Walking in a gale along the top of a thirty-mile-an-hour train as she sways and totters in the darkness, stepping over the three-foot abysses of death between the cars, we reached the warm haven of an empty ice box at the end of a refrigerator car, climbing down thru the little square hole in the roof.

Builders of railroad cars did not design those boxes for sleeping or living quarters. About 8 ft. by 7 ft. by 2 and one-half ft., with wooden gratings on the floor about four inches apart, they are not the most comfortable place in which four persons might spend a night. Springs, moreover, are not noticeably present as you bounce along in the darkness. But to us the place was a haven of refuge. Crowded like sardines we lay thru the night as we crashed northward. Now and then one turned over to extract a portion of his anatomy from the crevasse below, pulling an arm or a leg out of the grating it was trying to get thru. Or you requested the person on top of you to sleep a little more quietly.

For the convenience of the traveling public in general a reform in the methods of building ice boxes would seem to be imperative. And in considering general improvement, moreover, it would be well to provide greater publicity as to freight running times, and to strictly enforce the present schedules. It is slightly annoying at times for a gentleman to be forced to wait to midnight, say, as we had to, for a train due to leave at 11 o'clock.

At 7:30 A.M. we pulled into Tracy. As she began to slow up, the train vomited forth its weary travelers seeking to avoid the ever-noxious railroad bull. And what a horde we were. From "reefers," oil cars, and holes of various sorts I counted 17 piling out, and there were doubtless more. These were the hardier ones out of the army who awaited her at Fresno. Young, middle-aged, old, hobos, stiffs, yeggs, they were of every type that lead the restless life of the road.

Much of the traveling of these classes is done at night. Ditching is much less likely, concealment is easier. Sleeping in the daytime, moreover, requires no blankets, while one can shiver thru the night awake on a train.

It is a hard life, "a damn hard life," as our friend Smoke had remarked at Lindsay. Getting one or two meals a day, exposed to the chills and heats of night and day in a changing clime, cleanliness impossible, packed with others perhaps more unclean, traveling by night and sleeping when you can, the life leaves indelible traces on one's constitution even in a year or so, even without the dissipation usually constituting an important feature in the routine of the lives of this class. . . .

The freight was due to continue on to Oakland; a few went out ahead to board her again as she left. Most of the others, however, were bound for Stockton or the north. The three with whom I had sat at Selma, a strong, middle-aged man with an Irish face, and myself, decided to walk the twenty miles or so to Stockton.

After spending two days in Stockton hanging around itinerant gathering spots and talking with a variety of transients, Mills caught another freight north to Sacramento. He was particularly struck on this trip by the conversations taking place around him between his fellow travelers:

Sacramento, June 24th, 1:30 P.M.

A group of about 8 of us were waiting about a quarter of a mile out of town, most being young fellows without blankets. She pulled out at 7:50, going very slowly for about one and one-half miles out of town. We had no trouble at all in boarding her; I got on an oil car. There were about seven in the same place, between cars. All the way down the track men piled on, running out of side-streets, from behind culverts, tanks, etc. About 70 men in all got on, there being some on every car; some of the old-timers said that there were more there than they had ever seen on a single train. Some of them were young, some around 35–40, a few older. Quite a few I marked with Slavonic [*sic*] faces, foreigners speaking but little English, who boarded her. Of the whole gang not more than 10 at most had blankets.

As she still pulled slowly along the bunch began to fear being ditched. It was not yet dark; there were three shacks in evidence who watched the motley horde pouring on. It appeared that the shacks would sweep the train of every one on board within a short time, as it was too plain to pass unnoticed. The prospect of being forced to "unload" after she had got up speed was not enticing, and about 20 of the weaker brethren piled off. The majority, about 50, stayed with her.

Talk ran to trouble with shacks on trains. One boy of about 21, with an Irish face, of the city-street tough type, told of how a shack had attempted to throw him and one other off a train after she had got up speed. As it was going too fast they refused, whereat he attempted to throw them off. He was alone; the group was hidden between two cars. They grabbed him together and would have thrown him down between the cars if he had continued. He left them, however, and went back to the caboose, but soon returned with the whole crew of shacks. Discretion being the better part of valor in this case, the two "unloaded."

The necessity of staying out of the reach of shacks bearing lanterns was mentioned. Guarded with thick, heavy wire, these lanterns make nasty weapons, and are freely used by the shacks. The tale was told of one bo whose nose had been gashed and front teeth knocked out in this way, so that he was in the hospital for a week or so. Swearing vengeance if he had to stay there all his life, he waited till one evening the train was passing, the shack he was after standing on top of a car. With a heavy boulder he caught him a terrible blow on the head, almost knocking him off the car.

Soon a shack moved along the top of the train, and as he came to the oil car where a large group of us were stationed he had to crush his way thru the crowd, while they waited breathlessly to see what he might do. In austere dignity he moved straight thru and said nothing. The socialist crew out of Fresno could have done no more.

Soon the train stopped, and we scattered to look for better places to ride in. There were about 6 "reefers," all of which were already full. Finally we found two open stock cars, and in them most of us poured. There were at least 20 in the car I was in, sprawled on the dirty floor, or leaning against the sides. As we traveled more piled in, and the floor was soon so thickly strewn with dark forms that one could not move. Most of them were smoking cigarettes.

We pulled along very slowly, stopping frequently for long periods. One would have thought the hobo crew were traveling on first-class tickets by the way they cursed the train, mostly in good nature, however.

A most animated conversation was going on in the crowded car. The night was young, we were traveling, tho slowly, and a flood of wit, satire, and humor, coarse and otherwise, flooded and eddied around the dirty car. Some richly humorous remarks were passed. It was a veritable Hobo's Mermaid Tavern. One youth, between paroxysms of a racking consumptive cough, led in the thrust and parry of hobo retort courteous. His dad, he said, was a policeman in Waco, Texas. He had left home, vowing to his father that he would not have anything to do with any damned ——— of a ——— in his family that would wear a star. Somebody mentioned being hungry. "Why this hungry ——— of a ——— must have a tape-worm; here he ate the day before yesterday, and now he's talking about wanting another meal." As for himself, he said that he had had a cup of coffee that morning, and was good for a week or so. Last Fourth of July, he reminiscently stated, he had had 2 good meals.

Another told of having struck every passer-by on the main street of Stockton from 9:30 till 12 the night before, without getting a cent. Something was radically wrong with his "line," he guessed. Three bulls had previously told him to get out of town, so he was in hard luck. He had almost decided to go out and get hit by an automobile, so as to be taken to a hospital.

A story was told of an inmate of the Stockton asylum, a man who had a mania for digging wells. Digging one day near the gate, he got tired of his job and called in an Irish hobo passing, asking him if he wanted work. "What do you pay?" asked the hobo. "$2.50 and board," said the nut. "Good," said Pat and started in. He worked for half a day, delving out the hard clay ground. Then the keeper happened around and disillusioned

him. The nut's life was in danger for some time after that, it
was said. This well-digging nut was said to have become quite a
fixture around the place, offering various passers-by work at
good pay, but the news of him had become widespread, and no
more were taken in.

So the stories flowed, coarse and otherwise, but generally
richly humorous.

The talk fell to Sunny California, and it appeared that quite a
number of them were beating it East, having become tired of
conditions in this state. Most of these men were "tramps royal,"
having tales of conditions in nearly the whole country to recite.

The "bulls" of the northern part of the state were discussed.
It appeared that a good many towns were "Horstile." Roseville,
the Junction, was said to have a bad bull. A railroad cop had
been killed there a short time ago, and the present bull was sapping every one he caught in the yards. Yards almost impossible
to get out of on account of the high fence surrounding them.
One youth remarked that he would climb any fence in California if he had enough persuasion, and he was assured that he
would have it here. (Another remarked that when he was in the
army he would have shown them how to climb the fence.) Some
one said savagely that this bull would soon be killed too.

It was stated that at Auburn a vag caught near the tracks
would get 30 days right off the bat.

Soon it started to rain, and when we got to Brighton Junction, the jumping off place for Sacramento, about 5 miles out, it
was raining heavily. About half those on board got off and, a
weary crew, we headed up the track and the road. We soon
began to get soaked, and groups sought what barns and sheds
they could get to "flop" in. I struck a dilapidated shed whose
only virtue was that it was dry inside, spread my roll and
flopped.

After spending some time in Sacramento investigating employment
agencies and visiting IWW halls, Mills started north. After hitch-
hiking to Marysville and taking an uneventful train trip to Chico,
he decided to travel back south to Sacramento. He followed the pattern he was now used to and went down near the tracks to wait for
a train heading south. For the first time he had some difficulty in

catching a ride, but with perseverance he was able to make the trip.
Clearly he was becoming experienced riding the rails:

Sacramento, June 30th

That night I slept near the tracks, prepared to get up at a
moment's notice. One freight passed going south at quite a
speed, never stopping at all. In the morning, just as I got up,
the California Express came thru. I ran ahead, waiting to board
the blind, but the conductor rode it for about ¼ mile out.

After breakfast the manifest pulled thru. First I boarded a flat
car loaded with lumber, but a shack jumped on and told me to
"unload." I ran up ahead and boarded the "bumpers," but
another shack chased me thru and off, on the other side. Then I
waited and hit the rods, but after riding for a short ways saw a
shack waiting by the side of the train. So I "unloaded" before I
got to him. One man, I think, got her, climbing in on the
"blades" while she was stopped.

Things began to look pretty dismal. I thought of walking 25
miles to Oroville and getting the Western.

Talked at the station with two men, one about 40, one about
23, also bound South to Live Oak, where they knew a cook
who would give them a big hand-out. They had come up from
Marysville, where the bull had told them to leave by six o'clock
or he would give them six months, as he had found them drunk
in the jungles. They were bound for Fresno to get a "road
stake," then over the "hump" into Nevada, and thence to Kansas and the Middle West. Neither were of the excessively dissipated type, and both were still valuable workers. The older man
had traveled a good deal, but the younger was new to the game.

The south-bound local pulled out with about five cars, so
boarding her was impossible. However, I decided to follow her
about a mile down the track, where I heard she made up. The
others decided to follow me, after I had left.

Riding a local is rather to be avoided, as one may be ditched
at a little side-station, where the main trains never stop.

I got to her just as she pulled out, and as she had quite a
string of cars on her now I got on the bumpers. The other two
did the same. At the first stop we got off and opened a refrigerator car, into which we crawled. It was like an oven inside, mis-

erably and oppressively hot, a regular Turkish bath. We suffered till she started, when we opened the heavy doors a few inches.

Twice before we got to Marysville, a long trip, in the local, others pulled open the door and joined us. At Biggs a single, bloated bum came in, having come down from the north, a bum pure and simple. At Live Oak the rest got off, but two other knights of the road, also of the dissipated bum type, came in.

Riding in a refrigerator car is easier than on the rods or bumpers, but somewhat dangerous. The doors must be kept very nearly closed to avoid detection. If accidently, or on purpose, a shack should bolt the doors without, one would have a horrible death staring him in the face—in a dungeon with walls 8 inches thick, which never a sound could penetrate. However, one can watch the doors closely, and if on a long trip can see that the trap doors leading to the ice-boxes are unsealed. More than one unwary "gay-cat," (a road tender-foot) had been locked in these cars, however. Such cars are good riding in winter, as they can be easily warmed, as by burning several newspapers, and will retain the heat.

Got off at Marysville, and ate in a little restaurant where all the shacks and engineers were eating.

I had thought of staying with the local to Roseville, and then walking in, but as the walk was long and Roseville was somewhat "Horstile" I decided to go to Sac[ramento] on the Western. If there was no freight that afternoon, I would get the passenger at 2 A.M.

Went to the jungles and found practically the same bunch there as before, lying around reading and cooking, and boiling up. There are no regular meal hours in the jungles. One cooks up a meal at any hour of the day he may have the necessary scoffings.

Had a fine swim in the river, and coming back found an extra Western freight just coming in from the north. The gods were surely propitious. As she pulled thru, the jungles emptied themselves of many of their occupants. Putting on a coat, they were ready to travel to the world's end, with all their worldly possessions on their backs.

About 20 boarded her, some on the rods, some on the bumpers, some on oil cars. There were no empty box-cars or Gondolas. I got on the bumpers. We rode about 20 miles, then stopped at a little station some score of miles from civilization, called, I think, Pleasant Grove. The shacks came thru and kicked the whole bunch off, telling us to stay off. Pleasant Grove looked far from pleasant then. About 12 'bos were camped in a jungle in back of a ware-house.

The prospect of a stay there was not pleasing, so, as she pulled out, I boarded the rods, a place from which one cannot be kicked off unless she has stopped. One rod was loose, and the others were rather far apart, so the riding was not comfortable. There all the time, a foot below me and a few feet in back, rolled grim Death, ever following relentlessly after. A slip, a false move on the rods, ———.

With my bundle below one arm I made myself fairly comfortable till the next stop, about 8 miles distant. Then the head shack crawled down from the car above me. It looked like the Ditch for me, sure. "What are you riding on?" he asked, the customary form of address in such circumstances. Then "Where are you going?" I told him to Sacramento. "Well, stay off the rods or you'll break your neck," he said. As she started off he walked away, but turned and said, "Well, get on her." I thanked him, tho I was about to attempt to do so without the invitation.

All shacks are not the ogres one is apt to picture them. Few of them will ditch a man riding at night or riding out of sight. If a whole bunch ride together in plain sight there is no other course open to a shack but to ditch them. "Some fellows have no right to be on the road," a shack had said to a bum I had met. "They don't know enough to travel alone and to keep out of sight."

We pulled into Sac[ramento] at 5:30 with no further trouble. Starting off rather inauspiciously, I had been able to travel some 80–90 miles to where I wanted to go, so I had no complaint to make.

Mills's comment that shacks often allowed men to ride trains unmolested is an important one. His experiences led him to conclude that stereotypes about hostile trainmen were misleading. The customary form of address of a shack discovering a hobo on a train, "What are you riding on?," was a request for a union card identifying the rider as a worker. If an acceptable card was produced, the shack usually walked on.[3]

After arriving in Sacramento, Mills took a break from his hobo journey to visit Immigration Commission offices in San Francisco. On July 9 he returned to Stockton to begin what turned out to be the last part of his trip. He spent two days in Stockton, visiting the IWW hall and attending IWW meetings, and then started on a final round-trip to the north. He walked first to Galt, where he caught a train to Sacramento, then walked and rode trains to Marysville and on to Redding. Mills's last detailed description about rail travel concerned his trip from Marysville to Redding. He had particular difficulties in avoiding getting ditched on this trip but wrote again about the willingness of shacks to honor the identification of traveling workers:

Redding, July 21, 1914

Left Marysville on Saturday, July 18, at noon. Got the bumpers on a local freight. A shack came along after we were out a few miles, stopped and looked at me a minute quizzically, and asked where I was going. "Chico," said I. He walked on, and a few minutes later came back and told me to get into a gondola, one I had not seen before.

The train crept slowly along. I sweltered in the hot bottom of a steel gondola. At Live Oak, as we waited for a south-bound passenger, I got out and got a half-dozen cakes, the first food since breakfast.

At Gridley we had another long wait. I joined three other bums in an empty box car, two woodsmen, and a boiler-maker, according to their tales. The former were big men, strong, well-built, tho aging. The latter was a besotted little weakling, narrow close-set eyes, retreating chin, bedraggled black mustache, thin, weak frame—one of Nature's ruined vessels, surely. He had been up drinking the night before till the saloons closed at 3 A.M. The drinks he had got he had begged and sponged off others. He was just recovering now, belching what little food was in his stomach all over the floor, in the process. At a station where we stopped he begged a drink at a saloon, sick tho he

was. The fact that the saloon-keeper called him down properly
discomfited him not a whit. He spoke largely of his drunks, the
great and final proof of his manhood.

The train was slow, the car sweltering. As we waited at Biggs,
a thru freight came along (a manifest?). I found an excellent
place to ride in a great water-wheel, there being a small room
almost completely concealed from the outside. It had come thru
from Springfield, Ohio, consigned to Klamath Falls, and the
inner chamber bore traces, in the shape of scraps of food and
newspapers, of a shifting occupancy during the voyage. Apart
from an incessant clanking the riding was good, much better
than the walking at least. Stopped about an hour at Chico, but I
stayed in my hole, as I wanted to take no chances of getting
ditched. When we started up I saw another bum riding on the
rear of the car. As he had not seen my retreat, I called him in.

We rode in security thru to the Division at Red Bluff. At
Tehama we waited a long time, as something was broken. Heard
two shacks engage in a wordy war that almost resulted in a
fight, just outside our domicile. With a true hobo antipathy to
shacks, we chuckled happily at the event. Another shack came
by, glanced into the dark recesses of the water wheel, and
shouted, "Unload there, guy. Get the ——— Hell out of here. I
see you." We moved not, and he passed on, we laughing hugely
at the failure of his bluff.

Pulled into Red Bluff about midnight. I had had nothing to
eat since breakfast, except a few cakes, so I got out and hit for a
Chink restaurant. The crew from the train I had come in on
soon came in. Afterwards I went back to the railroad, crawled
unobserved into the wheel, and waited for the north-bound
freight to be made up. As the wheel was bound for Klamath
Falls, I knew it would go as far as Weed. Slept but a little, as we
were bumped around.

Just as we pulled out, at about 2 A.M., 6 others crawled in,
four young fellows, and 2 others, older. After we had gone a few
miles, the bunch smoking up on borrowed tobacco, we saw the
approaching lantern of the shack, as he combed the train for
bums. First he found two just outside the wheel we were in.
Came the inevitable question. "What are you riding on?" The
two attempted to explain, one showing a letter of some sort.

They failed to satisfy the shack, who ordered them to unload at the next stop. Then the penetrating rays of the lantern revealed five of us inside the wheel. In he came. "What are you fellows riding on?" None of us could answer. He asked if we had union cards. Most brakemen will let a man with a good union card ride at any time. They attempt to throw the shiftless hobo off, usually, but if convinced that a man is honestly after work many of them will let him ride. None, however, had union cards. The four young fellows explained that they had been unable to get food or work in Red Bluff, and were on their way to Portland. The second inevitable question came. "Any of you got anything on you?" Brakemen can often collect handy little sums from the multitude who travel on their lines. And most of them will play this game for all it is worth. None of us admitted having anything. It is a breach of the etiquette of the road to shell out for shacks. "Well, you fellows unload when we stop," he said, as he left.

Soon we drew up to let a southbound freight pass us. We waited for about ten minutes. Then two shacks appeared from the rear of the train, one the man that had come up previously. They said that the four young fellows bound to Portland could stay on, but ordered the rest of us to unload, asking us again, however, if we had anything on us. It was a lonely little switch, about 10 miles from Red Bluff, and we pleaded that it was a God-forsaken hole to be ditched in. The shack laughed, and said it was a pretty nice place. So we "unloaded." The shacks warned us not to try to get on again. One of them watched us for awhile, and when he left I walked back to look for a place to board her. I met two others who had been thrown off an empty because they would give the shack nothing. I had decided to hit the rods as far as Redding. Located a nice set of them, and lay down by the fence nearby, waiting for her to start up. Dawn was just breaking. Soon the shack who had thrown me off came by and spotted me. He came over and stood beside me with his lantern. "Think you're going to get on again, don't you?" he said. "Oh, I don't know," I rejoined. "If you do, you'll find it mighty unhealthy," he remarked. I was curious about his rates, and asked what he wanted to get into Redding (25 miles). "Six bits," he said. I laughed, and told him I could ride the cushions for that much. . . .

As the train pulled out he stood beside me. I remarked on the nice morning, and he said that this was a nice place, too. As she got up speed, I ran ahead, getting about 25 yards from him. Once well started, and I was underneath, he couldn't get to me till she stopped. As she gathered speed I boarded her. Tho the shack saw me, he was too far behind to keep me off, or to catch me. As the caboose reached him he boarded her, also. I thought I was safe, but looking ahead I saw a shack from the southbound freight, which had stopped while we went by, standing watching the rods. She was going fast, but I did not care to pass him and be jerked off, so had to unload. At least I consoled myself with the thought that the shack who had tried to hold me off thought I was on her.

Several others, who had also been ditched, were standing near. As a shack passed on top of the train he laughed hugely at the sight. One of the hoboes, a fiery young fellow, picked up a stone and heaved it at him. Tho it came nowhere near him, the shack pulled a revolver from his hip pocket, and fired four shots toward the group. His aim was probably not intended to be deadly, and the bullets went wild.

About 8 of us had been ditched. The switch was called Hooker. Not a house in sight. It was said to be 8 miles to the nearest water tank. We surely had been "hooked."

I decided to walk to Cottonwood, about 8 miles away, trying to get there in time to board the Oregon Express, due to leave Cottonwood in about one and one-half hours. One other, an Austrian, I judged him to be, came with me, but the rest decided to return to Red Bluff, only 10 miles away, while Redding was 25.

We hit out, walking at a brisk pace. The sun rose, as we walked. After about 4 miles a freight thundered past us, a shack on top waving gleefully at us, and laughing uproariously.

The gods were with us, for just as we reached Cottonwood, the first section of no. 16 drew in, stopping for just a moment. During that moment we boarded the blind, and started gaily forth again. At Anderson a crowd at the station saw us, but we were unmolested. We drew into Redding at about 6:30, and

were forced to jump off in the midst of a crowd who were waiting for the train, who evidently enjoyed the sight immensely. I
dodged the bull, whom I saw stalking near. Washed off a considerable layer of dirt at a faucet on a nearby lawn, where about
15 hoboes were sleeping. My one regret was that the freight had
just gone thru, so that I could not gloatingly show myself to my
friend the shack.

After a short stay in Redding, Mills took a train back to Sacramento
where he ended his hobo journey. Part of the appeal of life on the
road to Mills was that every day brought new experiences. Each of
the train trips he described was different. Each trip presented new
challenges—either getting on, staying on, hiding from shacks, ne-
gotiating with shacks, staying warm, or getting where he wanted to
go.

III

Besides describing his personal experiences, Mills also wrote
about incidents he saw or heard relating to life riding the rails. Train
stories were a standard topic of jungle conversations, and he recorded
tales and incidents that impressed him. Common themes included
the dangers of travel by train, run-ins with hostile bulls and shacks,
and incidents in which hoboes got the upper hand over authorities:

Stockton, June 22, 10 A.M.
The kid told of several tramp experiences his cousin had had
in Montana. Once in a box car two hold-up men had gone thru
a bunch of tramps, holding them up by the light of burning ker-
osene poured on the floor. Another time a fellow hobo had
made himself persona non grata to the shacks on a freight, who
were prohibited by law from throwing him off a moving train.
They promised two others a ride for as long as they wanted if
they kicked him off. Accordingly, as he was standing near the
door, one swung to his head, while the other kicked him, and
the last they saw of him he was sliding down the rocky road
bed, alive or dead they knew not. . . .
He reported that the country around Manteca was "horstile,"
and that both county and railroad bulls were "sapping" all
hobos they caught near trains. ("Horstile" is an interesting

word. Doubtless derived from hostile, it is pronounced entirely
differently and has a specific and distinctive meaning of its own.
A "horstile" country or railroad is one where people—bulls or
shacks—are working to get rid of hobos, stiffs, etc.). . . .

Marysville, July 17, 1914

Fight this A.M. on the Western.

12 hoboes in an empty— Conductor comes to them—"Get
out of there, you ——— ——— ———." One says, as he gets
out, "There ain't none of us here that answer to that name."
"Aw, you're all a bunch of lazy bums," says the Con. The 'Bo
retorts, "Why, I've got a union card as good as yours any day."
"Well, it ain't no better," says the Con, and swings his heavy,
wire-protected lantern, cutting the hobo's scalp severely. Whereat some of the 'boes ran, while others stood and fired rocks at
the train crew. One of the shacks had his head cut, it was
reported. This at 4 A.M. this morning.

Accidents are frequent on the road. One shack was brought
into Roseville with arm and collar-bone broken, one side of head
crushed. He had tried to throw a hobo off a train, and both fell
together, the shack underneath.

Sacramento, July 24, 1914

In the morning met a boy of about 17 who had just lost $30.
Pocket picked by tramps on top of #15. The two of us got into
conversation with an ex-shack, one who had railroaded and
bummed all over the United States. He told of spotters for the
railroads who ride as bums to see if trainmen take money.
About 8 years ago in the Siskiyous a spotter disappeared. This
man told of where he had gone. A train crew had caught him
one night on their train and recognized him. Took him to the
engine, a coal-burner, opened the furnace door and threw him
in. Another spotter was found cut in two on the track one
morning.

At noon saw a very interesting sight. Shasta Limited came
into Red Bluff at about 12 o'clock. I was waiting for her, hoping
for a chance to get out on her. As she lay there, the engine right
in front of the station and the crowded main street, two hoboes
deliberately and openly climbed onto the cow-catcher. The con-

ductors came up, looked into the blind, and started back. A crowd of people were watching, and laughing, but said nothing. When the engineer was ready to go, and tried to release the brakes, the air failed to work. The two hoboes had turned the air-cock. After a minute or so, an excited conductor, fireman, and brakeman ran to the front of the train, and ejected the two with much cursing. They sauntered back, and, as she slowly started up, both commenced to "deck" her. The train slowed up, while the conductor and brakeman ran back after them. They got down, only to board the next car. By this time the whole train crew was on the one side of the train, holding these two off, so finally she was able to pull out without them. The crowd watching the hoboes had thought they must be crazy. Soon they came over to where a bunch of us were sitting, and explained that a pal of theirs had to get out of town on that particular train. By their ruse he had been able unobserved to "deck" her on the other side, making the Shasta out in the middle of the day—no small feat.

The leader of the two was a rather tall, stout fellow, loud-mouthed, with a colossal nerve. He wore a dark suit, and a hat such as small-town marshals are wont to affect. Beneath his coat he wore a fake policeman's badge. He delighted in telling how he worked this badge. At Eugene, Oregon, he had walked up to a shack, who had just ditched a small army of hoboes— told the shack that he was the town marshal, that he had ordered all bums out of town, and that the shack was to let them ride. He himself was to ride with them to see that they got out. The whole army rode south in triumph, the pseudo-marshal their honored chief.

The juxtaposition of violence and humor in this last journal entry is startling. In placing the story of the death of the railroad spotter just before the slapstick incident of the two hoboes getting their friend on the Shasta Limited, Mills was not trying to be dramatic. These contrasting incidents illustrate what Mills meant when he said there was "a strong, virile, pulsing beat of reality" to existence on the road that got into your blood.[4]

7

Observing the IWW

June 22, 10 A.M.
Scribbled around Stockton railway station—"I.W.W. Join the
I.W.W."

I

In his journal and in the reports and papers he wrote after his
journey, Mills referred again and again to the impact of the Industrial
Workers of the World (or Wobblies) on California's casual laborers.
The IWW was such a major force in contemporary California that
its presence intruded constantly into his remarks.[1]

By 1914 the Wobblies had been in California for nearly ten years.
Founded in 1905 in Chicago, the IWW was one of the most dramatic
manifestations of the "Age of Industrial Violence" in the United
States. Although ostensibly a union, the IWW was a syndicalist organization unlike the craft unions of the American Federation of
Labor (AF of L). While the AF of L worked within the system and
attempted to acquire for its members a larger share of the wealth
created by capitalism, the Wobblies aspired to replace capitalism with
a new world of worker control. Rejecting collective bargaining and
business unionism, the IWW welcomed conflict, and in the United
States of the early twentieth century it found a fertile ground for its
message. In its years of peak activity before World War I, the IWW
led strikes across the nation among millworkers, lumberworkers,
steelworkers, and miners. Strikes at Paterson, New Jersey, and Lawrence, Massachusetts, in particular gained national attention.[2]

Initially the IWW was an urban organization in California, but
local chapters were set up in agricultural districts starting in 1909.
Over the next five years, the union rose from relative obscurity to

an organization known by every aware citizen in the state. First with the urban-centered Fresno and San Diego free speech fights of 1910–12 and then with its role in the Wheatland hop fields riot of 1913, the IWW became feared and opposed by respectable opinion throughout California. Through the publicity generated by these actions, the union managed to transmit its message to almost every itinerant worker in the state. Because of the IWW's focus on the problems of the most exploited and hopeless laboring groups, many itinerants began to see the union as the only defender of their interests.[3]

Although Mills opposed the IWW's message of "direct action" through conflict and strikes, since the major purpose of his journey was to observe forces affecting itinerant workers, he tried to assess opinion about the union. As a result, his notes provide a rare glimpse of views held by migrants and itinerants about the Wobblies.

II

Mills found evidence of the presence of the IWW everywhere he traveled. One ubiquitous sign was the messages left on "hobo bulletin boards," as Mills called them:

A point worthy of note in this regard is the numerous references one sees concerning the I.W.W. Perhaps it is only the three letters engraved on the seat of an out-of-the-way station house. Or it may be the name of an I.W.W. organizer. Again it may be a sentence [such] as "Join the I.W.W.—Eight hours work." The extent and activity of this organization's workings are almost beyond belief. One sees the notices everywhere. You hear the "Wobblies" spoken of favorably in "jungle" conversations. There is a widespread knowledge of and interest in its doings that is of far more than passing importance in any consideration of the problems connected with this organization.[4]

The impact of the IWW was also evident in the fact that almost everyone Mills met had an opinion about the union. His journal reports many of these comments:

Dinuba—May 31—5:30 P.M.:
[Conversation with two itinerants]

We talked of work in general, of the Japs, of the canneries at
Selma, where conditions were said to have been very bad till the
I.W.W. cleared them up.

Minkler—June 3, 1914
[Conversation with young hobo from Chicago]

He didn't have a "Wobbly" card as he said, but his sympathies
were strongly with them. He had sold their papers in many
cities jumping in gratuitously. "The Wobblies get four bits of
every dollar I have if they want it," he said enthusiastically. Like
most of the brethren of the road, tho not himself a Wobbly he
admired them immensely. The hoboes realize that the I.W.W.
generally picks on a pretty rotten situation and clean[s] it up,
and [they] have a genuine respect for them. This boy told me
that he had been fired from one peach-picking job for some
"Wobbly" talk in regard to poll taxes. He stated that all
employers of seasonal labor would stamp immediately on any
I.W.W. tendencies in camp.

Sacramento, June 24, 1:30 P.M.
[Conversation while walking with hobo toward Sacramento]

He spoke strongly for the I.W.W. Said they were making a
great fight in a big cause. Thought there would be trouble in the
hop fields this fall. Said that Durst would get "his" soon, in
addition to losing his barn. Believed that Ford and Suhr ought
to be free.

Ralph Durst was the owner of the Wheatland hop ranch where
the August 1913 riot took place. Ford and Suhr, Wobbly spokesmen
at the Durst ranch, were found guilty of the deaths that occurred
during the riot. As a result of the Ford-Suhr decision, the IWW
planned a hop fields strike in the fall of 1914 (which was not successful) and a demonstration at Wheatland in August (which took
place as scheduled, but without incident). Mills heard about these
plans repeatedly during his trip:[5]

Marysville, June 27, 12 Noon

I was told that there was no work around here or in the north. Was handed an I.W.W. protest dodger. All the men around here seemed to be in sympathy with the Wobblies. Ford and Suhr were said to have been very unjustly treated. It was said that the Porto Rican did the shooting, the jungles were plastered with I.W.W. posters.

Most of those here seemed to think that a strike on hop-picking would not be a success. They said, that the hoboes would not pick, but that the families would do so. The burning of Durst's barn was favorably spoken of. One remark caught my attention. Some one spoke of the District Attorney having been killed, meaning Manwell. Another said "Why, I didn't know he had been killed *yet,*" thinking the remark referred to the present District Attorney.

Not everyone that Mills met supported the IWW. He referred to several such incidents:

Marysville, June 26, 1914, 4:40 p.m.

I led the conversation to hops and the I.W.W. Of all the bums I have yet talked to, these are the only ones to curse the Wobblies, and curse them they did. They blamed them for all the trouble; Durst, they said was a kind-hearted man, and would feed every man that applied, bar none. They stated that the hop strike was bosh, that hops would be picked, all right.

Sacramento, June 30th

Talk ran to the I.W.W.'s. For the second time since I have been out I heard them condemned. A man of about 50 spoke bitterly against them. Said that in Portland last winter they had taken charge of the distribution of food and blankets, given by charity, and had kept the lion's share, and the best of everything for themselves. Then they had boasted of having kept the poor all winter. (A certain Tabernacle had been kept open in Portland.) This individual believed that a few hundred hoboes would refuse to pick hops, but that thousands of people, especially families, would be willing to do so.

Marysville, July 17, 1914

Picked up by a farmer, with a curious rising inflection as he spoke. Spoke of very bad times. Hay $7 a ton, formerly $15.

Blamed Wilson and the Democrats, entirely. Said that men could not be secured who would keep jobs for more than a day or so. Classed I.W.W.s as anarchists. Said that the militia would make them keep order in the hop fields.

Marysville, July 17, 1914
  Picked up by pedlar, and rode with him thru Rocklin and Loomis, to within one mile of Penryn. Pedlar (who was also a small farmer) hated the I.W.W.

Redding, July 21, 1914
[Waiting for train to Redding, talking with railroad guard]
  Then, to find out what his attitude towards the I.W.W. might be I asked if a Wobbly card was good to ride on. "Not worth a damn," he said.

Mills's reports on his investigations of the orange and lumber industries expanded upon the divergent appeal of the Wobblies to different groups of workers. In Lindsay he found that "there is no form of union among these orange workers and practically none of them, so far as I could learn, have I.W.W. or Socialistic affiliations or tendencies. They do not appear to be of a type readily susceptible to unrest agitation, while the nature of their work and the organization of the industry itself, make unionism of any kind extremely difficult." With respect to the lumber industry, Mills wrote:[6]

  The strong animosity of the employers toward labor organizations of all kinds has been mentioned. This feeling has a counterpart among many of the lumber-jacks themselves, tho here it is not so much a feeling of animosity as one of distrust, coupled with a belief that they have no need at all for them. The reason is found largely in the nature of the men themselves. Strong, independent, self-reliant, they are accustomed to stand on their own feet and make their own demands. If a lumber-jack is dissatisfied, he says nothing but gives up his job, leaving for another camp where, as a skilled man, he knows he can get work. He does not want this personal freedom interfered with thru his being linked to others probably weaker than himself. From the conversations I have heard, I judge, too, that they rather distrust unions from the scandals that have developed in connection with some of them. Living apart, moreover, from the active world for most of the year, they appear to take little interest in such things. Tho I have heard some socialistic talk in a quiet way, no virulent form of social unrest appears to be cropping out here.

What has been said above applies distinctively and primarily to the lumber-jacks, the woodsmen proper. The men in the mill are of a different type in general and more than once union talk has been started here. The type, not quite so independent and self-reliant, is more susceptible to union ideas, and the employers are constantly on the lookout for any out-cropping of this nature. From the talk I heard in the valley from various hoboes and other I.W.W. sympathizers, I know that the latter organization is anxious to organize these mill and lumber workers, a partially successful attempt having been made in the North. To the present, however, no headway has been made in this region and prospects are not bright for any organization of this nature in the near future.[7]

Mills's comments provide two insights into the impact of the IWW in California by 1914. The first is that everyone had an opinion about the organization. In his conversations with railroad guards, hoboes, farmers, orange packers, lumberjacks, and dozens of others, he found that everyone knew about the IWW and had taken sides on it. The second insight Mills provides is that distinct labor groups responded differently to the Wobbly message. Those associated with the employer class (farmers, railroad guards) were opposed to the IWW. Skilled workers (lumberjacks, orange packers) also tended to be unsympathetic. The IWW had its strongest support among the unskilled and the disaffiliated—the lowest groups in the hierarchy of labor. Even among these groups Wobbly support was not universal (there were two cases in which Mills heard the IWW cursed by hoboes), but support at this level was widespread and often vehement. He commented on this aspect of the appeal of the IWW in a paper entitled "The Hobo and Migratory Casual on the Road" and in his journal:[8]

The evidences of a social unrest, of a growing dissatisfaction with their lot in life, are not lacking among this class. The appeal of I.W.W. principles is the most alluring of all the voices that offer a way out, and there is a wide-spread knowledge of and sympathy with the activities of that organization. It is worthy of note that it was not the hobo class, usually very conspicuous in the hop-fields, who broke the plans for a general hop strike, in the fall of 1914. The I.W.W. itself is in California notably an organization of itinerants.[9]

Sacramento, June 30th

I.W.W.ism is simply one attempt to find a way out. Many others on the road feel that something is wrong. Some think syndicalism offers the remedy. But most of them feel the need of change, be what it may. No change, of course, can make their position worse; here, perhaps, lies the most dangerous element in the whole situation.

Mills concluded that the IWW message was embraced by most migrant workers because of the hardships of itinerant life. Comments about the difficulties of a life on the road appeared throughout his journal:[10]

Sacramento, June 24th, 1:30 P.M.
[Walking from Brighton Junction to Sacramento]

The condition of the two I had walked up with may be imagined from this incident. It was raining heavily, their coats were pulled up over their huddled shoulders, as the rain soaked thru them. It was past midnight, no shelter was near, and town was four miles away. As we passed an orchard an electric arc light showed apricots lying scattered on the ground beneath dripping trees, inside a high barbed-wire fence. Without hesitation they crawled thru it and fell to eating and stuffing their pockets with the fruit. I passed along, not caring to wait, and left them out of sight. Later they came for a moment into the barn, but found it so open and uncomfortable that they decided to continue—
If only your stay-at-home economists and social philosophers might have seen that little midnight scene it might have jolted out of them some of their notions as to the excellence of the present economic system.

Mills was not alone in feeling that the appeal of Wobbly ideas to many itinerants was understandable. Paul Brissenden, a fellow Immigration and Housing Commission investigator, concluded in a

"Report on the I.W.W. in California" that the IWW was a reaction to a system of treating itinerant labor that was "socially bad" and "socially antiquated." Peter A. Speek, one of the primary Industrial Relations Commission investigators, stated in an October 1914 report that the distress of the unemployed in San Francisco was so great that Wobbly speakers attracted larger crowds than any other organization. Speek said that "their speakers are encouraged and applauded by the crowd. I am impressed that they will play an important role among the unemployed multitude in the coming winter. The distress of the unemployed and the influence upon them by the I.W.W. may lead to riots." Carleton H. Parker also found the impact of the IWW message on itinerants to be understandable. In an article on the IWW published in November 1917, Parker argued that "the I.W.W. [is] purely a symptom of a certain distressing state of affairs. The casual migratory laborers are the finished product of an economic environment which seems cruelly efficient in turning out human beings modeled after all the standards which society abhors." To Parker, the itinerants' interest in the Wobblies was "a natural psychic outcome of a distressing and anti-social labor condition."[11]

III

During the time that Mills was traveling, the IWW was active throughout the Central Valley and had locals in most larger towns. At one point his journal recounts at length a conversation with an IWW recruiter:

Stockton, June 23d, 9 A.M.

In the morning as I stood by the station before breakfast, I was hailed by a small man in overalls, seedy grey coat, and battered hat—weasel-like grey eyes, a trifle bleary, with a week's stubble on his face, who was sitting on a truck. I joined him, and we talked for about 20 minutes. He asked me where I was bound and where I had come from, asking me for information about the I.W.W. local in Fresno. He was an I.W.W. "card man," and had just come down from "Sac," where he said there were all sorts of bums. They were everywhere, however, he said, so it did not matter where one went. He gave me several of the hop stickers in English, Japanese, and Chinese. There were about

4,000 card men in California, he said, and 500 in the three Sacramento locals alone. I stated that I was going north to the hop country, and he said that I wanted to be careful about picking hops. I reassured him, telling him I merely wanted to see what was doing. He stated that there would be lots of card men in the fields this fall.

We spoke of Durst's barn being burnt, and he intimated that "four of us" had been in on it. Ryan, the watchman, he said, was an old I.W.W. card man, in spite of his assertions to the contrary.

He told of a trip he had made to the north, telling how he had picked up a friend who had fed him on booze for a week, tho the friend himself did not want any. Traveling on a freight a shack had asked him what he was traveling on. "I'm traveling on a red card," he had said, defiantly. The shack had assured him that that was all right, and they had ridden unmolested. He had finally got his friend to purchase a card, $1 for a card (initiation), 50 cents a month dues, and 25 cents for the Ford-Suhr fund. The man had given him $5. Of this he had sent $4 to headquarters, for, as he said, "I had to get some pay for my trouble." He hinted that I might also get a card, but I excused myself on the grounds of poverty.

He gave me some information about freights to the north, and said the "Mail" was good riding.

Of the Ford-Suhr appeal pending, he said that three of the five judges were "all right," and thought a new trial would be granted.

As we parted he said, "Stay away from Durst's ranch. Some bastards are going to get killed up there this season."

He was one of the lesser pawns in the great labor game being played on the coast. None too intelligent or too moral, yet imbued with an enthusiasm for his cause, he was putting all his time into the "war of the workers against the masters," into the attempt to break down the law of the Masters.

During the last part of his journey, Mills spent much of his time around Wobbly halls whenever he was in a town. His sketches of these encounters have a liveliness seldom captured in formal studies. Mills mentions three visits to IWW locals in his journal and also refers to his IWW card. He joined under the name of Fred Carr (IWW card No. 183352, showing dues paid for July, August, and September 1914, and an assessment stamp for the defense of Ford and Suhr):[12]

Sacramento, July 13th, 1914
  Reached Stockton 5 o'clock, July 9th. After supper went to I.W.W. local. Asked for "Shorty," but did not find him. Explained that I had told Shorty that I would take out a card thru him, but was prevailed upon to take a card from the secretary, a tall, thin-mustached Irishman named Connellan, who introduced me to the group in the room as "Fellow Worker Carr," after I had paid the necessary money. As an honest workingman they shook my hand, and said that they were glad to see me in the fight. Connellan classed me as a "Construction Laborer" on the card.
  Went up to the square to help start their meeting, walking up with a young fellow named "Shorty," whose face was decorated with an embryo mustache of a blonde hue. He told me of their general plans for Wheatland. With us also walked another Fellow Worker, a youth of about 22, with a startling lack of intelligence.
  Found two rival meetings in the square. One was being addressed by "Dare-Devil Devlin, the crippled globe trotter," and one by a bunch known in the vernacular as "Jesus screamers." After the singing of a few I.W.W. songs, Smoky Jones, said to have been a veteran of many free-speech fights, addressed the crowd. Smoky, a rather uncleanly, unwashed specimen, with very bad teeth, I had seen at the hall. His common talk was a mass of high-flown phrases. When at the hall someone had spoken of the difficulty of getting freights, Smoky had said that he believed the time would come when the bums would simply sit down in a town and refuse to move. "Why should they endanger their lives stealing rides?" But when Smoky got on a stump, then was his cup of joy full. High-sounding phrases, words of learned length and rumbling sound, combined in various forms to constitute an unparalleled flow of verbiage. The commonest statement must needs be twisted and transformed into a weird and wonderful thing. But withal Smoky got by with the crowd.

His talk dealt largely with the damnable idiocy of the A.F. of L., and of all craft-unions allowing themselves to be used as they were in Stockton, where open shop had just been declared.

Next came Marcus A. Otis. He stood up, coatless, in a red shirt, well built, strong face—the typical laboring man of the full-dinner-pail type. Strongly, forcibly, emphatically, he delivered his message, with a ringing earnestness that drove it home to the soul in spite of the coarseness of some of his remarks. It was the old tale, the foolishness of the working classes, the producers of all things, who lived as slaves. In a telling, gripping style he delivered his talk. Once he said: "You people think you live, don't you? You think you are happy. Well, answer just one question, and answer it truthfully. Will every married man in this crowd raise his hand? Come on, stick your mud-hooks up." There were about 200 present, all mature working men, most of them of the casual class. The crowd was with him, and, I am inclined to believe, answered him truthfully. Not a man raised his hand, tho the question was repeated several times. "Well, do you call that living?" he went on. "Even the black chattel slave had a chance to propagate his race. You men don't know what it is to have a home, a wife, a child, and yet you think you live. Think of that the next time you go up to Annie's room to buy yourself a home on the installment plan."

It is not idle discontent that these men preach, not vapid, idle words that they use. It is revolution, bloody revolution, and some of their arguments are bitterly unanswerable. As yet it is but talk, largely, but Ludlow, Paterson, West Virginia, Wheatland are not meaningless phenomena that can be safely ignored. . . .

I flopped that night on the grass behind the hall. About midnight I was awakened by some bum who asked if he might flop with me. Unkind as it was, having only one blanket, I was forced to deny him, for the sake of safety and cleanliness.

Jungled with the bunch in the morning. They had all slept around the place, on the floor, on benches, etc. Shorty and I walked to a bakery and got a sack-full of snails [coiled pastries] and doughnuts for 25 cents. With coffee this made a meal.

The lock-out and strike [were] discussed, and the foolishness of craft-unionism condemned. The weakness of trade and craft unionism is beginning to be understood, even by craft-unionists themselves.

Wrote to Doc in the morning, sitting in some wheat sacks. Talked with a working man who said that the union would never get anywhere till they all got together.

Hung around the hall in the afternoon. Connellan and another fellow worker sang I.W.W. songs with infinite gusto and enjoyment.

Otis and Smoky Jones both spoke again that night. (Friday, July 10th) A special appeal for money for Ford and Suhr was made, and $5 worth of stamps sold. Remarks of all kinds in favor of sabotage were applauded by the crowd. Literature was given out free to the value of the money collected.

I left a little early with the secretary, who told me more of the Wheatland plans. (He is chairman of the "agitation committee." There is such a committee in each local.) I left that night. Was given a bunch of stickers and some blanks to fill out about jobs, and organization opportunities. Secretary wished me luck.

Flopped in the hay stack out of town where I had flopped while in Stockton before. Had a fine sleep.

Sacramento, July 13th, 1914

Walked into Sac[ramento] on Sunday, July 12th, and went down to the I.W.W. hall. Secretary said no jobs on hand. Walked up with the boys to the afternoon meeting. Heard Carl [Carleton H. Parker] damned right and left. (They had had a joint meeting of the three Sacramento locals that morning with only 12 present, the other 588 members being out of town "on the job.") Scott, Downing, and Edwards spoke, largely on Wheatland.

Saw Brissenden in the hall later. Went to the evening meeting. Heard Dare-Devil Devlin give a good talk. Some religious fanatics were carrying on at the same time, a motley crowd of men and women, white and colored. While the Dare-Devil had a large audience, these people were their own audience.[13]

Redding, July 21, 1914

Found an interesting secretary in the I.W.W. local—a hale, hearty man, 70 years of age. He had taken part in many a fight already, he said, and hoped to be able to take in many more. Planned to go to Wheatland if he could. Would work privately there, saying nothing of what he did. He stated that the present wage-slavery was worse than the black chattel slavery. (He had been raised in the South.)

He looked for a crisis this winter in the impending conflict between capital and labor. Said conditions were getting worse all the time.

He allowed no one to join this local who did not thoroughly understand and swear by the principles of the I.W.W. He kept the place in order, keeping the bums and drunks out.

Met two interesting types last night. One Carrigan, Wobbly, just out of jail where he had served five months. One, Mac-Namara, a member at large of the I.W.W. Formerly W.F.M. [Western Federation of Miners] member. A traveling agitator. Hair, straggly, red; beard and mustache, straggly, red; face strong as so much granite. Eyes deep sunk, burning with the fire of a strong will and a fiery enthusiasm. Beetling eyebrows, red. Strong chin. Face almost haggard in the lines of force it showed. Speech, strong, savage, biting, tho uncultured. A rabid and radical direct-actionist. . . .

The camaraderie of the I.W.W. was well illustrated at Redding. The fierce MacNamara threw 50 cents on the table for the secretary, then asked if anyone in the room had not eaten. Gave 50 cents to one man who said he was hungry. Then invited the bunch out to drink.[14]

The above descriptions provide a rare glimpse of daily events at Wobbly locals. The visits on which these comments are based also resulted in the most vivid of all Mills's remarks concerning the IWW. In an untitled paper he wrote his strongest personal statement about the militancy he felt emerging around him among California's disenfranchised laboring classes:

Redding—July 20th
————I am living eating and breathing agitation, agitation that is really anarchy. More than ever I feel the force of the great social unrest that is boiling and seething on the underside of the thin crust upon which the whole social fabric rests. Now and

then it breaks thru in a small eruption, but on the whole we ignore it. It is easy to say that the conception of any such dangerous discontent is imagination, it is so vague and strange to us. I felt it vaguely at first, then strongly when I came into personal contact with members of a great floating army, homeless, unmarried, denied any of the joys of life, over half of the millions in this army of casuals dying before they are forty years old. And I feel it vividly and keenly now. I have seen, to a very limited degree, some of the workings of the inner circle, the brains of this great army, the organizing force that is trying to tell this army of its strength, trying to teach them how to get their share of the goods of this world. And the message they bring, the message millions of men are listening to, is one of violence, bloodshed, "Direct Action" they call it.

This sort of talk is old; we have heard it all before. But what astounds and grips one is the enormous number of men by whom this method is accepted as the one way of escape from a life as deadly and painfully miserable as that of a bond slave. In city squares the thought is applauded; in hobo jungles it is endorsed. Upton Sinclair, Jack London are preaching it. And if the thought is ever successfully transformed into the deed, we'll have some pyrotechnic displays in this country that will make the French Revolution look like child's play.

Incidently the IWW are planning a campaign of violence in the hop fields this fall that promises trouble. They expect to have 2,000 men at Wheatland on August tenth (even the date is set) prepared to go to any lengths to free Ford and Suhr. The fact that the State is prepared for trouble will probably prevent anything serious occurring, but there are possibilities of excitement. Tho one feels that he is playing with fire all the time, it is a great game to have a hand in.[15]

The impersonal, objective style with which Mills began his reports on his hobo journey had disappeared by the time he wrote this statement. He was deeply impressed by the "dangerous discontent" he felt around him. Yet, in the same paper immediately following this statement, he recounted one of the most humorous episodes in his journal:

Redding—July 20th
There are low lights as well as high lights, humorous as well as
tragic incidents in this world of the submerged. In a square at
Sacramento two rival gatherings were fighting for the public ear
one Sunday evening. On the one hand were some religious
fanatics, "Jesus Screamers" as the Wobblies term them (the blas-
phemy is not mine). On the other side was an IWW meeting. A
joint meeting was out of the question, so it was up to one of
them to drive the other away. As a campaign measure the religious meeting started loudly bellowing hymns. Unknowingly
they were playing into the hands of the IWW, for the latter have
their own words to the tune of almost every popular hymn. So
the war started. "In the sweet bye and bye" floated across.
Immediately 200 stentorian male voices were lifted in song.

> "You will eat bye and bye
> In that wonderful land in the sky,
> (Tenor—Way up high)
> Work and pray, live on hay,
> You'll eat pie in the sky when you die.
> (Basso—That's a lie)"

Tho drowned out, the religious people carried it thru. Verse for
verse the IWW met them. One of the verses rendered by the latter was particularly appropriate.

> "Holy Rollers and Jumpers come out,
> And they sing and they dance and they shout,
> Give your money to Jesus they say,
> He will cure all diseases today."
> Chorus—"You will eat bye and bye" etc.

The "sky-pilots" then started another song. "When the roll is
called up yonder"—. Came the male accompaniment from across
the street—

> "When the Holy Rollers wander
> When the Holy Rollers wander
> When the Holy Rollers wander (When you buy a job out
>   yonder)
> When the Holy Rollers wander (When the driver yells 'Roll
>   out, boys.')
> I'll be there."

At the end of this song, in which the religious sect was completely drowned, I looked for an unconditional surrender on their part. But they were made of sterner stuff. The devoted band came forth with, "Hallelujah, Amen" etc. Back rolled the bass burden:

> "Hallelujah, I'm a bum,
> Hallelujah, bum again,
> Hallelujah, give us a hand-out
> To revive us again."

(A hand-out is the technical hobo term for a meal "handed out" to him at a farm, a residence, a restaurant, etc.)

That squelched them completely, as far as singing was concerned. They called a policeman, who put it to a vote of the crowd as to which they desired to hear, the result being unanimously in favor of the IWW. One negress refused even to give up at this juncture, enlivening the whole meeting with shouts of "Glory to God," etc. It was a famous victory for the Wobblies.[16]

At first glance, Mills's statement "I am living eating and breathing agitation" seems incongruent with his recounting of the "battle of the hymns" incident. Upon reflection, however, their pairing is a perfect way to summarize what he found on his hobo journey. Mills was dealing with real people and real lives in his travels, not abstractions or stereotypes. The people he met got wet and cold on midnight tramps and stole apricots; they packed oranges for twelve hours a day and then went home to cook and keep house; they bummed around town squares in packs; they planned strikes and they burned barns—they had humor and they had pain. Mills's July 20 entry illuminates the humanity and the complexity of the life he observed as effectively as any statement ever written about the IWW or about itinerant labor problems.

8

Conclusions

The recognition of an acute social problem in migratory farm labor, a problem so serious as to shake the foundations of the State, which the Wheatland Riot and the appearance of General Kelley's Army had forced upon the people of California, was, unfortunately, destroyed by the World War. Both incidents passed into history. Even the beginning toward a solution of the problem, as indicated by the creation of the State Commission on Immigration and Housing, was soon nullified. Reactionary postwar administrations proceeded to undermine the work of the commission . . . and the blind chaos of former years once more prevailed.

I

Frederick Mills's hobo journey took place during a brief period of intense popular interest in the problems of itinerant workers. The public spotlight rarely lingers long in one place, however, and as Carey McWilliams indicates in the quotation above, the focus of attention soon shifted to World War I.[1] As a result, although some important advances were made (most notably in labor camp sanitation), little was done in California to change, in a basic way, the lives of seasonal and migrant workers. For the public, everything soon changed in terms of issues of interest. For the people Frederick Mills met and lived with on his two-month journey, everything remained much the same.[2]

II

In late July 1914 Mills reported to the San Francisco office of the Immigration and Housing Commission. He was assigned other duties and did not return to the Central Valley as a hobo. Over the following year he conducted investigations of employment agencies, urban lodging houses, and conditions in labor camps. No records of this work survive in his papers except for a letter of recommendation summarizing his contributions written by George Bell, attorney and executive officer for the commission, upon Mills's departure from the commission in August 1915.[3]

Mills entered the graduate program in economics at Berkeley in September 1915 and completed a master's thesis the following spring. During the next five years, he finished his Ph.D. at Columbia University, served in the American Expeditionary Forces in France, got married, and returned to Columbia as an assistant professor. As his personal and professional interests evolved over these years, he began to concentrate on issues other than those of his hobo days. But as his later work on his novel indicates, he never forgot his two months on the road.

Mills does not say in his papers why he stopped his field investigations at the end of July 1914. Carleton H. Parker's wife, Cornelia, in a biography of her husband, implies that Mills came down with malaria. The end of his trip also coincided with Parker's preparation of testimony for the U.S. Commission on Industrial Relations hearings in August. Mills's records contain paragraphs that were reproduced in papers submitted to the commission, so it is likely that his help was needed in preparing these reports.[4]

Parker's testimony at the August 27 session of the CIR hearings in San Francisco summarized statistics from Immigration Commission collections of life histories of itinerants and data from investigations of labor camps. Based on these studies, Parker later developed a theory of the psychology of the casual worker, which he presented at length in a 1915 article entitled "The California Casual and His Revolt." These issues remained the focus of his professional work up to his death during the flu epidemic of 1918.[5]

After Mills returned from his hobo trip, the Commission of Immigration and Housing directed its efforts for the rest of 1914 to processing the information collected during the intensive investigations of the previous months. The CIH prepared an annual report and a special *Report on Unemployment* and implemented plans to deal with problems that required immediate attention according to its studies. In October 1914 in the midst of these actions, Parker resigned from his position as executive secretary of the Immigration Commission. His departure was not an amicable one, and it originated from dissatisfaction on his part and on the part of other members with the commission's progress.[6]

After 1914, with Parker gone and the Immigration Commission's initial fact-finding activities completed, the commission's work took a new direction. Governor Johnson assigned to the commission the responsibility for finding the cause of a series of rural fires. With this step, the field investigations of the commission moved from data gathering to labor espionage. Mills and other early investigators had not served as labor spies. In a sworn affidavit submitted to the State Department in 1955 as part of a passport application, Mills discussed his hobo days and explicitly denied that he was an "undercover agent." According to Mills, the purpose of his trip was solely "to study living and working conditions among migratory workers in the state." The term labor spy, however, became an accurate description of Immigration Commission agents in the years that followed. This was particularly true during World War I, when commission investigators apparently spent more time reporting on the antiwar activities of the IWW and in trying to convince workers not to strike than on their ostensible duties of investigating labor camp conditions. The result was a rapid decline, after 1914, in the effectiveness of the commission in dealing with its initial mission—the improvement of living and working conditions of itinerant workers.[7]

Like the Commission of Immigration and Housing, the U.S. Commission on Industrial Relations and the IWW soon ceased to be effective voices for reform. The Commission on Industrial Relations failed to reconcile the wide variety of views about seasonal labor presented at its San Francisco hearings into a set of recommendations for action. It dissolved in August 1915 under a cloud of controversy that included a three-way split among its members over policy recommendations. All three groups within the CIR acknowledged the distressingly high level of bitter and open conflict between labor and management in the United States but disagreed in their analyses of the crisis. The various recommendations of the commissioners received wide publicity, and several bills were introduced in Congress, but little was accomplished because World War I soon commanded the nation's attention. Many of the commissioners' recommended policies were eventually implemented—a minimum wage, the eight-hour day, greater progressivity in the tax structure, and government support for collective bargaining—but these advances were the result of intervening events rather than the work of the Industrial Relations Commission.[8]

The effective role of the Industrial Workers of the World as an advocate for migrant workers ended on September 5, 1917, when a series of coordinated raids across the country by agents of the U.S. Justice Department stripped bare IWW centers. In the weeks that followed federal agents arrested hundreds of IWW members. The reason for this dragnet was the IWW's vehement opposition to U.S. involvement in World War I. The Wobbly position that workers should refuse to fight in a war between the ruling classes was not tolerated by a government committed to support of the Allied powers. Vestiges of the IWW lingered after 1917, but it ceased to be a major social force.[9]

Without help from state or federal governments, the seasonal workers and itinerants Mills met on his trip were left to survive as best they could. In the years that followed, the orange industry underwent changes in the transportation and storage of fruit, but the fruit still needed to be picked and packed by hand, and the labor of seasonal workers was still required. The lumber industry underwent a technological revolution in the 1920s with the introduction of the internal combustion engine as a substitute for the steam engine—the donkey engine eventually disappeared as the chain saw and diesel tractor took its place—but again the seasonal nature of the work remained. The story was similar for road construction; the tools and techniques changed, but the irregularity of employment remained a constant. Migrant agricultural workers experienced perhaps the fewest changes in their lives over the ensuing years. There were some important developments: with the growing popularity of the automobile, families rather than single men became a common sight in the fields, and rapid technological change increased the output of workers dramatically. But thousands of seasonal workers were still needed, and the living and working conditions of agricultural migrants changed little.

The massive numbers of itinerant workers of Mills's day, however, gradually disappeared in the following decades. As the manufacturing and service sectors replaced agriculture, lumbering, mining, and their attendant processing industries as major employers, the proportion of workers in seasonal jobs declined. With population growth, local workers were available for jobs once filled by itinerants. The eventual development of social security, welfare, disability, and unemployment insurance programs also reduced the need for workers to tramp. The unemployed and homeless remained, but they usually lived year-round in cities, and they no longer periodically flooded urban areas during recessions and winter months in the way that had so concerned middle-class citizens in the early twentieth century.[10]

III

When Mills took his trip, he could not know that the period of intense interest in migrant issues would be brief. He also did not know that the influence of the organizations that played key roles in creating this moment—the California Commission of Immigration and Housing, the U.S. Commission on Industrial Relations, and the IWW—would be equally short. During the years that followed, Mills became aware that little of substance resulted from the investigations he had been part of in 1914. When he returned to his hobo notes during the 1950s and adopted the approach of writing a novel based on his experiences, he used his story to comment on this outcome.

Mills's novel is important because in it the mature Mills was free to reflect upon the ultimate value of his hobo journey. Through the story of hoboes Ben (Mills) and Red, he emphasizes three central themes. The first one is the importance of detailed knowledge about the life of migrants. Mills judged correctly that the careful observations and accurate descriptions of itinerant life summarized in his novel were the major contributions of his journey.

The second theme in Mills's novel is developed when he breaks into the story of the travels of Ben and Red to visit an economics seminar at Berkeley led by a fictional Professor Rogers. He uses this literary device to show the lack of understanding about migrant life outside of the working class. The implication in this section that misinformation was a barrier to public appreciation of the plight of migrants is an accurate commentary on the entire history of the homeless in the United States.

The seminar includes several students, Professor Rogers, and an unemployed boilermaker from Oakland named Groller. Tom Rivers, one of Rogers's students, presents the standard theory of labor markets with its optimistic conclusions about labor mobility guaranteeing that unemployment will be temporary. Mills then has the boilermaker respond to these assertions:

"Well," said Groller, "this has been quite an experience for me, Professor Rogers. I've learned a lot, though not about the labor market. I'm quite a believer in books. I'm not an educated man myself, but I've read a lot and have learned a lot from books. But I've found out this afternoon how dangerous books can be. Books tell you something about the world you live in, but even the best books leave out a hell of a lot. Some books leave out everything. Take labor mobility. That's a nice phrase. I suppose Mr. [Rivers] has learned from books how men bargain for a job, how they save enough to keep them and their families happy between jobs, how they know all about jobs and pay, and how they move, by Pullman I suppose, to where the jobs are fattest. My God, doesn't he know these drifters he spoke of are the men who do most of the hard work in California? They harvest the wheat, pick the fruit, fell the trees, build the roads, the dams, the bridges, cut the tunnels, mine the ore. While they're on a job, they work sore—I wonder if Rivers could learn from a book what that means—to work until every damn muscle and bone in your body is aching, until you don't mind the wet, lousy clothes you fall asleep in. And when the job gives out they're mobile all right! That reserve fund they had bargained for when they took the job doesn't quite cover travel by Pullman. So they grab a rattler, or climb to the deck of a passenger. Sure, they'll be sapped and ditched, but there's always another train to give them mobility again. Or their feet. Full knowledge of the demand! Sure. A passing stiff will tell them there's a job on construction near Tehama. Another heard a jungle report of haying near Bakersfield. But the bulls may be horstile if you go there. In Texas, though, they say there are lots of jobs at good pay. And the employment agency! Take a job there, and it'll probably last two days, till you've covered your transportation. Then out on your ear, and a new man pays his slave market fee. And your family, that you're going to keep happy between jobs! The one thing he can be thankful for is that he hasn't got a family. These men aren't married. They couldn't be, and still be mobile, Mr. Rivers. Some may have left wives in Peoria, but the others never had wives, and never will."[11]

The points Groller makes in this statement summarize effectively the important misunderstandings about itinerant life that impressed Mills on his journey.

The third theme of the novel is presented in the last section of the book, where Mills focuses on the futility of policy debates among those in power. He felt that the failure to respond to the glaring problems facing itinerant workers needed to be a main theme of his novel. The conclusion of Mills's novel is also of interest because it echoes real events. He tells the story of a meeting of citizens in San Francisco concerned about mass unemployment during the winter months. The group most likely had as its inspiration the Commonwealth Club of California, which formed a committee in the summer of 1914 to investigate the problem of unemployment in San Francisco. Similarly, several of the statements made before this fictional meeting can be found in testimony before the Industrial Relations Commission in San Francisco in August 1914, and the policy suggestions that it debates are similar to those proposed by the Immigration Commission and Industrial Relations Commission: Should the government support a system of public employment agencies and regulate the fees of private agencies? Should it develop a plan for diversifying the state's industries to reduce seasonal swings in the demand for labor and create a state program financed by a bond issue to provide work for the unemployed in the winter? Mills used the response of his fictional Professor Rogers to the group's vote on these recommendations to comment on contemporary policy debates:[12]

The discussion continued for half an hour, with the tide of opinion running heavily against the Committee's proposals. A few voices supported the recommendations. Mrs. Ralph Harrison, a social leader, spoke of the degrading conditions under which migrant workers lived. The Reverend Walter Chase warned against the negative attitude that seemed to prevail, and pleaded for some positive measures. But although there was general sympathy with the Committee's objectives, the concrete proposals were considered unacceptable. The final votes, recorded by a show of hands, showed 63 Ayes and 128 Noes.

Chairman Grey announced the result with a serious face. "It is a matter of deep regret to me," he said, "as I am sure it must be to many others who are here, that the work of Mr. Hill's devoted committee has come to naught. This cannot be our community's last word on the pressing problem that faced us this winter, and that we will face again. We must all hope that in time we shall achieve understanding and win through to a just solution."

At this point a note was handed to him from the audience. Mr. Grey read it, and then announced, "It was my intention to adjourn the meeting at this point. However, one of our guests from across the Bay, a distinguished student of the subjects with which we have been grappling tonight, has requested the privilege of the floor. This I am happy to extend. I now introduce Professor Joel Rogers of the University of California."

Professor Rogers walked quickly to the front of the room and mounted the dais. He opened in a somewhat tight voice. "Mr. Chairman, Ladies and Gentlemen. Two months ago I attended another meeting concerned with the problem that was discussed here tonight. It was held in Union Square. Those in attendance were the unemployed of San Francisco. Many ideas were expressed, ranging from appeals for violence and a thinly veiled invitation to class warfare to a sober appeal for cooperation with the authorities. The upshot was the misguided march on Washington and its disgraceful ending under the firehoses and the clubs of armed deputies. The impression I carried away from that Union Square was of confused men, lost before a problem that was too big for them. There was frustration, confusion, uncertainty, fear, all overlying a bed of misery. There was honesty there, too, and goodwill, but these were lost in the fog of doubt and bewilderment.

"I have listened intently to your discussion tonight. I shall carry away much the same impression—an impression of men lost before a problem that is too big for them. The misery that underlay the Union Square meeting you are spared—whether by your own merits or the grace of God. But confusion, uncertainty, doubt, and fear—they are all here. And there is honesty and goodwill, too, but they appear lost, as they were in Union Square. The net result of both meetings, in my mind, is despair.

For they point in the same direction, down a road that is dark and gloomy, that we must follow with foreboding.

"I would not argue that the recommendations you have rejected offer a final solution of this great problem. Perhaps they are not the best we could do; they are doubtless far from perfect. But they are something—a beginning—and we could learn by trying them. The alternative you have chosen, the negativism of complete inaction, is morally indefensible. And the grounds for it—the bonds might not be a triple A investment, the state might take over all industry if it told men where work was to be had! If a man were rescued by collective action from an avalanche or an earthquake—such an earthquake as we had here a few years ago—his moral fiber might be weakened! These are not arguments we can be proud of.

"More than half a century ago Thomas Babington Macaulay made a fateful prophecy about the future of the United States. When there was no longer a frontier said Macaulay, to absorb the discontented and the unemployed, America would be rent by class war. Its prosperity would be destroyed by demagogues bent on despoiling the rich. Then we should move in one of two directions. The republic would be laid waste by its own barbarians, or some Caesar or Napolean would seize the reins of government. Well, the frontier has gone. The men who are here tonight were in the last great wave, the wave that reached the western shore. Yours, most immediately and personally, is the problem. Shall we be rent by class war? Are Macaulay's two paths to be the only ones open to us? I think not, if we bring reason to play on our social problems, and solve them with justice as they arise.

"You believe, and I believe, in the democratic system, the system that guarantees individual liberty and ensures human dignity. Can this system, on its economic side, be made to work without the loss of that liberty and dignity, without the human wastage we have witnessed this winter? I think it can. I am sure it can. We have a rich and fruitful system. It will be richer and more productive. But its fruits must be widely shared, and it must do so with a full sense of social responsibility. Otherwise we must face the possibility of class war, and all that that could mean to the democratic tradition, to human rights, to the

potential of life on earth. We have seen that specter this winter.
God grant that it may never take on substance in this country
of ours!

"You have spoken tonight with mixed tongues. There have
been expressions of good intentions on all sides, even on the
part of those who have argued against and voted against the
modest trial steps proposed by your committee. But to express
goodwill is not enough. This alone will not cope with the social
sickness that afflicts us. If this is all the citizens of San Francisco and of California can do, under the challenge you face
today, then the world may fairly say, "Woe unto ye, Scribes and
Pharisees, hypocrites."

There was some clapping, largely lost in an angry murmur
that swept the room as Professor Rogers took his seat. John
Grey stood at the speaker's table, silent, until the murmur died
down. Then, "I declare the meeting adjourned."

In contrast to the vote in Mills's novel to defeat reform proposals,
the real Commonwealth Club did agree on a set of recommendations
to help alleviate the distress of the unemployed. Nevertheless, Mills's
decision to end his novel with futile arguments over policy recommendations was an ideal way to summarize the final impact of the
multitude of goodwilled but ineffective committees and commissions
of his day.

Mills correctly highlighted the main themes of his hobo record:
the importance of accurate information on itinerant life, the lack of
understanding about that life, and the inability to implement adequate policy. His novel, journal, and reports provide a perceptive
record of life among the floating army of hoboes, itinerants, and
seasonal workers who walked the roads and rode the rails in early
twentieth-century California.

Notes

Introduction

1. Frederick C. Mills, "E-6," 9. Since Mills's papers are mostly in draft form and include occasional punctuation and spelling errors, repeated words, and crossed-out phrases, for clarity I have corrected most of these errors silently in this book. For the origin of the terms describing itinerant workers in the quotation see Joyce L. Kornbluh, *Rebel Voices: An I.W.W. Anthology*, 67.

2. Mills's focus on rural areas and small towns in his investigations was determined by his supervisors on the Immigration Commission. See the letter from Carleton H. Parker to Simon Lubin, May 15, 1914, Lubin Collection, Bancroft Library, University of California, Berkeley, and Parker, "Unemployment and the Migratory Worker," 1–2. An account of the urban dimensions of vagrancy in Mills's time is in Kenneth L. Kusmer, "The Underclass in Historical Perspective: Tramps and Vagrants in Urban America, 1870–1930," in *On Being Homeless: Historical Perspectives*, 21–31. Important studies of itinerant and migrant labor that provide a context for Mills's trip include Parker, *The Casual Laborer and Other Essays*; Parker, "The California Casual and His Revolt"; Nels Anderson, *The Hobo*; Carey McWilliams, *Factories in the Field: The Story of Migratory Farm Labor in California*; and Vardon Fuller, "The Supply of Agricultural Labor as a Factor in the Evolution of Farm Organization in California," 19,777–898. Recent studies of hobo life include Kenneth Allsop, *Hard Travellin': The Hobo and His History*; Roger Bruns, *Knights of the Road: A Hobo History*; and Douglas Harper, *Good Company*. Recent studies of California farm labor include Lloyd Fisher, *The Harvest Labor Market in California*; Cletus Daniel, *Bitter Harvest: A History of California Farmworkers, 1870–1941*; Linda Majka and Theo Majka, *Farm Workers, Agribusiness and the State*; and Anne Loftis and Dick Meister, *A Long Time Coming: The Struggle to Unionize America's Farm Workers*.

3. The rise of the underclass in the period after the Civil War is reviewed in Kusmer, "The Underclass," 21–31; and Michael B. Katz, *Poverty and Policy in American History*, 157–65. The accounts of hobo life cited are Walter Wyckoff, *The Workers: An Experiment in Reality*; John J. McCook, "Leaves from the Diary of a Tramp"; Josiah Flynt, *Tramping With Tramps: Studies and Sketches of Vagabond Life*; and Jack London, *The Road*. Other firsthand accounts of hobo life include Charles E. Adams, "The Real Hobo: What He Is and How He Lives"; Theodore Waters, "Six Weeks in Beggardom"; and James Forbes, "The Tramp; or, Caste in the Jungle." For an account of how hobo life changed in the decades after World War I, see Eric

142   NOTES TO PAGES 2-9

H. Monkkonen, introduction to *Walking to Work: Tramps in America, 1790–1935.*

4. Contemporary observers of the underclass who were simultaneously sympathetic and judgmental include Wyckoff, *The Workers,* and Jacob A. Riis, *How the Other Half Lives: Studies Among the Tenements of New York.* Mills's sympathy for the itinerant workers he met is suggested by the fact that he almost lost his job with the commission. The labor representative on the commission thought he was "too radical, almost in sympathy with the I.W.W." See Peter A. Speek, "Notes on the Situation of Migratory Laborers and Unemployment in California."

5. For early attitudes toward tramps see Katz, *Poverty and Policy,* 157–65; Daniel T. Rodgers, *The Work Ethic in Industrial America, 1850–1920,* 226–29. Robert Hunter, *Poverty,* 63–64; and W. Jett Lauck and Edgar Sydenstricker, *Conditions of Labor in American Industries: A Summarization of the Results of Recent Investigations,* 172–73. Also see Anderson, *The Hobo,* 267–68; Herbert G. Gutman, "Work, Culture, and Society in Industrializing America, 1815–1919"; Katz, *Poverty and Policy;* Alexander Keyssar, *Out of Work: The First Century of Unemployment in Massachusetts;* Kusmer, "The Underclass"; Monkkonen, ed., *Walking to Work;* David Montgomery, *The Fall of the House of Labor: The Workplace, the State, and American Labor Activism, 1865–1925;* Rodgers, *The Work Ethic in Industrial America.* Frederick C. Mills, *Contemporary Theories of Unemployment and of Unemployment Relief.*

6. Mills, "The Orange Industry of Central California," 14. Mills, "E-6,"

7. Mills's emphasis on the pressures on workers to degenerate is not common in recent analyses (Kusmer, "The Underclass," 21, 26, is an exception), but it was common in Mills's time. See Hunter, *Poverty,* 131; Lauck and Sydenstricker, *Conditions of Labor,* 171; and Peter A. Speek, "Report on Psychological Aspect of the Problem of Floating Laborers: An Analysis of Life Stories," 37–62.

Chapter 1. The Wheatland Riot, Kelley's Army, and F. C. Mills

1. For discussions of the Wheatland incident see Carleton H. Parker, "The Wheatland Riot and What Lay Back of It"; Woodrow C. Whitten, "The Wheatland Episode"; Melvin Dubofsky, *We Shall Be All: A History of the Industrial Workers of the World,* 294–300; Kornbluh, *Rebel Voices,* 227–29; Joseph A. McGowan, *History of the Sacramento Valley,* 106–12; David F. Selvin, *Sky Full of Storm: A Brief History of California Labor,* 33–36; and Daniel, *Bitter Harvest,* 84–99. Photographs related to the Wheatland riot can be found in Richard S. Street, " 'We Are Not Slaves': The Photographic Record of the Wheatland Hop Riot; First Photographs of Protesting Farm Workers in America."

2. Living conditions in migrant labor camps are discussed in California Commission of Immigration and Housing (hereafter California CIH), *First Annual Report.*

3. For an account of the march of Kelley's Army, with photographs of the confrontation between the army and the police in Sacramento, see E. Guy Talbott, "The Armies of the Unemployed in California." Also see McGowan, *Sacramento Valley*, 112–16.

4. Parker, *Casual Laborer*, 62.

5. The centrality of labor conflict in the first two decades of the century is affirmed in Melvin Dubofsky, "Abortive Reform: The Wilson Administration and Organized Labor, 1913–1920" in *Work, Community, and Power*; and in David Montgomery, *Workers' Control in America: Studies in the History of Work, Technology, and Labor Struggles*. For other studies that focus on labor violence in the United States around the beginning of the twentieth century, see Sidney Lens, *The Labor Wars: From the Molly Maguires to the Sitdowns*; Graham Adams, Jr., *Age of Industrial Violence, 1910–15: The Activities and Findings of the United States Commission on Industrial Relations*; Louis Adamic, *Dynamite: The Story of Class Violence in America*. For broader perspectives on violence in America see Richard E. Rubenstein, *Rebels in Eden: Mass Political Violence in the United States*; Irving J. Sloan, *Our Violent Past: An American Chronicle*; Richard Hofstadter and Michael Wallace, eds., *American Violence: A Documentary History*; Hugh Davis Graham and Ted Robert Gurr, eds., *The History of Violence in America: Historical and Comparative Perspectives*; and Charles Tilly, Louise Tilly, and Richard Tilly, *The Rebellious Century: 1830–1930*. The comment about the viability of a free society is in Adams, *Industrial Violence*, 228.

6. The quotation stating the original intent of the California CIH is in a letter from California Governor Hiram Johnson to Simon Lubin, first president of the CIH, dated August 20, 1912, in the Lubin Collection. For a history of Johnson's role as governor and leader of the progressive movement in California, see George E. Mowry, *The California Progressives*.

7. The CIH quotation is in California CIH, *First Annual Report*, 15. A March 30, 1914, version of Parker's *Report on the Wheatland Hop-Fields Riot* is in the papers of the U.S. Commission on Industrial Relations. A June 1, 1914, version almost identical to it is included in Parker, *Casual Laborer*, 171–99. A preliminary version is in Parker, "Wheatland Riot," 768–70.

8. For Parker's background, see the biography by his wife, Cornelia Stratton Parker, *An American Idyll: The Life of Carleton H. Parker*. Details of Parker's career after he left the CIH in 1914 also can be found in Robert E. Ficken, "The Wobbly Horrors: Pacific Northwest Lumbermen and the Industrial Workers of the World, 1917–1918." The order by Governor Johnson to investigate the Wheatland riot is discussed in Samuel Edgerton Wood, "The California State Commission of Immigration and Housing: A Study of Administrative Organization and the Growth of Function," 184. Parker also worked for the U.S. Commission on Industrial Relations in his investigation of the Wheatland incident. See "Correspondence Relative to Wheatland Riot Trials Held at Marysville, California, January 1914." Parker's con-

clusions about the causes of the riot are presented in Parker, *Report on the Wheatland Riot;* Cornelia Stratton Parker, *Idyll;* Parker, "California Casual"; and Talbott, "Armies of the Unemployed."

9. The quotation about the thirty-five reports is from Wood, "Commission of Immigration and Housing," 143. Parker, "California Casual."

10. The list of titles of the thirty-five reports is in California CIH, *First Annual Report,* 115–17. The two reports reprinted in California CIH, *Report on Unemployment* were "Life-History Statistics" and "Employment Agency Situation in California." According to Parker's biography, he hired two former students who "hoboed it till they came down with malaria, in the meantime turning in a fund of invaluable facts regarding the migratory and his life." Cornelia Stratton Parker, *Idyll,* 83. The other former student was Paul Brissenden, who later wrote one of the first major studies of the IWW. For a summary of Parker's efforts in setting up the staff of the CIH and a list of those working for him see Parker, "Unemployment and the Migratory Worker," 1–2.

11. Information about Mills's life was obtained from clippings, letters, and memorials in Mills's papers. Also see *Current Biography, 1948,* s.v. "Frederick C. Mills" (New York: H.H. Wilson, 1948), 453–54; and the memorial to Mills in *Political Science Quarterly* 79 (September 1964): 480c-d.

12. Mills's doctoral dissertation was published as Mills, *Contemporary Theories of Unemployment and Unemployment Relief.*

13. Mills told his mother, Lily Mills, about the book of her poems in his letter to her of August 25, 1932. Mills's poem, "Of Friday and Edie and Ayres," appeared in the *Journal of the American Statistical Association* in December 1937.

14. The comment on the Roosevelt administration is in a letter from Mills to Eli Ginzberg, March 2, 1934. Mills's objection to nuclear weapons appeared in a letter to the editor, *New York Times,* February 16, 1946. The exchange with Simon Kuznets is in letters from Mills to Kuznets, April 19, 1927, and Kuznets to Mills, April 20, 1927. Mills gave Juan-Ruiz Magan permission to translate his statistics book into Spanish in a letter dated March 14, 1932. In 1944 Mills heard that Magan had been imprisoned for being a member of the Masons. See Mills to Ruth J. Perry, May 17, 1945, for Mills's work with the American Friends Service Committee to help Magan. Mills's former student William Remington was charged with disloyalty in 1948. Mills's efforts on Remington's behalf are chronicled in letters from Mills to Remington, August 14, 1948, February 23, 1949, and July 31, 1951. Remington lost his case, and eventually died in prison.

15. Mills's main contribution to the methodological debate was "On Measurement in Economics." His comments on pragmatism are in a letter to Robert Mills, June 29, 1957. Mills's early claim that economic knowledge was "statistical" was in "On Measurement."

16. The offer from Berkeley came in a letter from Ira Cross to Mills, March 2, 1920. The university's disappointment in his decision to stay at Columbia was voiced in Cross to Mills, March 19, 1920. His comment on his pref-

erence for the East is in a short autobiographical statement dated May 12, 1942. Mills's statistics book became a standard text and was translated into six languages. His comment about the prisoners of war is in an undated letter apparently from the early 1960s headed "Dear Max." The selection of Mills's book *The Behavior of Prices* as one of the best social science contributions of the 1920s is discussed in Raymond T. Bye, *Critiques of Research in the Social Sciences.*

17. For the history of agriculture in California, see Ralph J. Roske, *Everyman's Eden: A History of California;* Majka and Majka, *Farm Workers;* Fuller, "Supply of Agricultural Labor"; and Daniel, *Bitter Harvest.* For a graphic contemporary statement about California's need for cheap, temporary labor see R. L. Adams and T. R. Kelly, *A Study of Farm Labor in California,* 7–8.

18. The U.S. Commission on Industrial Relations (CIR) hearings took place on August 27 and 28 in San Francisco and are recorded in vol. 5 of the commission's *Final Report,* 4911–5085. That Parker wanted Mills's help in preparing reports for the CIR is indicated by the fact that pages 7–8 and 16 of Parker's "Preliminary Report on Migratory Labor in California" were apparently written by Mills. Mills's papers contain drafts of several paragraphs that appear on these pages. Mills's work with the CIH is summarized in a letter of reference from George L. Bell, attorney and executive officer of the CIH, September 29, 1915.

19. Parker, "California Casual," as reprinted in Parker, *Casual Laborer,* 80. Lauck and Sydenstricker, *Conditions of Labor,* 150, 173. John A. Fitch, "Old and New Labor Problems in California," 610.

20. The data on manufacturing employment are taken from the United States Department of Commerce, *Statistical Abstract of the United States: 1916,* 264.

21. Mills, "E-6," 5, 8. Basing its conclusions on several surveys of tramps around the turn of the century, the characteristics of the tramping population are discussed in detail in John C. Schneider, "Tramping Workers, 1890–1920: A Subcultural View."

Chapter 2. "Rustling" Oranges in Lindsay

1. Letter from Carleton H. Parker to Simon Lubin, May 15, 1914, Lubin Collection.

2. Mills's comment about the purpose of his trip is in Mills, "The Hobo and Migratory Casual on the Road," AA. This is an important statement because soon after Mills's trip, field agents of the commission began a policy of labor espionage, focusing on the activities of the IWW. Wood, "California State Commission of Immigration and Housing," 263, dates this transition as occurring early in 1915. The most active of these labor spies was J. Vance Thompson, who was hired in 1914 over Parker's objection. For Thompson's career and his work with the CIH, see Bruce Nelson, "J. Vance Thompson,

the Industrial Workers of the World, and the Mood of Syndicalism, 1914–1921." In 1955, as part of a passport application, Mills reaffirmed the purpose of his trip in a sworn affidavit. According to Mills, "I was assigned, during this period, to study living and working conditions among migratory workers in the state of California. . . . As part of my assignment, I joined the Industrial Workers of the World, and held membership for a period of about two months. I did so neither as an advocate of militant industrial unionism nor as what is now termed an 'under-cover agent.' No criminal issues were involved. The purpose of the [commission] was to ascertain facts concerning the living and working problems of migratory labor." The affidavit is attached to a letter from Mills to Mrs. R. B. Shipley, Passport Office, Department of State, dated April 7, 1955, Mills papers. Mills's statement about the job announcements is in Mills, "E-6," 9.

3. The communications between Mills and the CIH are in the Lubin Collection. Two postcards from Mills show that he kept the commission office apprised of his activities. A copy of a wire from Simon Lubin giving Mills direction in his investigation indicates that communication took place in both directions. A letter from Mills's sister to the commission implies that Mills wrote his report on the orange industry immediately after leaving Lindsay while he was still on the road. Mills mailed the report to his sister, who typed it and submitted the final copy to the commission. Mills's comment about his hobo disguise is in Mills, untitled report beginning "Case 1-," Mills papers, b.

4. Mills, "Case 1-," Mills papers, b.

5. For the history of the Lindsay area, see William Wilcox Robinson, *The Story of Tulare County and Visalia*. A survey of the history of the orange industry in California can be found in Vincent Moses, "Oranges for Health—California for Wealth: The Billion-Dollar Navel and the California Dream." Moses focuses on Southern California, but he does discuss briefly the development of a seasonal labor force in the industry by the early 1900s.

6. Mills, "E-6," 10, 11.

7. John Steinbeck, *The Grapes of Wrath*. William Duffus, "Labor Market Conditions in the Harvest Fields of the Middle West," December 1, 1914, 21, 41. Also see Peter A. Speek, "Report on the Preliminary Investigation of the Harvest Hand Situation in the States of Kansas and Missouri."

8. Mills, "E-6," 11.

9. All quotations headed with dates are from a typescript of Mills's daily journal, entitled "Record," Mills papers. The description of the work in Drake's is in Mills, "Record," entry dated May 22, 1914, and in the report Mills submitted to the CIH on his investigations, "The Orange Industry of Central California." He also submitted a shorter report on orange picking entitled "A Supplementary Report Concerning Orange Picking Conditions."

10. Mills, "Record," May 22, 1914.

11. The IWW and its impact on itinerant workers are discussed in chapter 7. A radical organization intent on destroying the capitalist system, the IWW had been in California since shortly after its founding in 1905. It was not

until 1909 that local chapters were set up in agricultural districts. By 1914, after the Fresno and San Diego free speech fights of 1910–12 and after the Wheatland riot of 1913, the IWW was near its peak of activity and influence in the state. The activities of the IWW are surveyed in all major California histories. Another investigator for the Immigration Commission, Paul Brissenden, wrote one of the first studies of the IWW, *The I.W.W.: A Study of American Syndicalism*. For an evaluation of Brissenden's contribution and a review of other early studies of the IWW, see Dubofsky, *We Shall Be All*, 531–32. See Dubofsky for a recent comprehensive history of the IWW, and Kornbluh, *Rebel Voices*. Specific studies of the IWW in California include Hyman Weintraub, "The I.W.W. in California, 1905–1931"; and Ione E. Wilson, "The I.W.W. in California with Special Reference to Migratory Labor." Daniel, *Bitter Harvest*, also analyses the IWW's impact on migrant labor.

12. Mills, "E-6," 13.

13. Ibid., 17.

14. The estimate of 4,600 people in the orange-packing industry is in Mills, "Orange Industry," 2. Mills's estimate of the numbers of workers in other seasonal industries is in Mills, "E-6," 2, 5. Parker, "California Casual," in *The Casual Laborer*, 80.

Chapter 3. Work in a Sierra Lumber Camp

1. Mills, "Record." Journal entries are indicated by a heading giving the date of the entry and are not otherwise noted.

2. The history of the lumber industry around Hume is covered in Lizzie McGee, *Mills of the Sequoias*. Also see Marion A. Grosse, "A Century of Lumbering in Fresno County," in *Fresno County Centennial Almanac*. Photographs of the area and excerpts from McGee are included in Ralph W. Andrews, *Redwood Classic*. Logging techniques of Mills's time are described in Richard L. Williams, *The Loggers*. Mills, "An Economic Survey of a Sierra Lumber Camp," 1.

3. Ibid.

4. Ibid., 3.

5. Ibid., 23.

6. Mills, "Scenes and Incidents 'On the Road,' " 10–11.

7. Ibid., 13–14.

8. Samuel Baily, "The Adjustment of Italian Immigrants in Buenos Aires and New York, 1870–1914," 304–5; Herbert S. Klein, "The Integration of Italian Immigrants into the United States and Argentina: A Comparative Analysis," 328–29.

9. Williams, *The Loggers*, contains descriptions of logging camp life that are similar to Mills's. Mills's evaluation of the conditions at the camp is contained in Mills, "Survey of Lumber Camp," 14–17. The wages of the

men are given on pp. 18–19 of the same report. Parker's estimate of an average thirty-dollar winter stake is in Parker, *Casual Laborer*, 121.

10. Mills, "Survey of Lumber Camp," 9–10.

11. Ibid., 4.

12. Ibid., 8.

13. Ibid., 10.

14. Ibid., 9–10.

15. Ibid., 19–20.

16. Ibid., 21–22.

17. For a discussion of dual labor markets, see Richard C. Edwards, Michael Reich, and David M. Gordon, eds., *Labor Market Segmentation;* and Michael J. Piore, *Birds of Passage: Migrant Labor and Industrial Societies,* 35–43.

18. Parker's estimate is in Parker, *Casual Laborer,* 69. Mills's estimate is in Mills, "E-6," 5.

Chapter 4. The Employment Agency Game

1. "Hindus" were Asian Indian workers.

2. Mills, "The Sand Creek Road Situation." The information in the following three paragraphs about work on the road gang is taken from this report.

3. Parker, "Preliminary Report on Migratory Labor in California," 2–3. Also see Parker, "A Report on Employment Agencies in California."

4. William Leiserson, "The Labor Market and Unemployment," 34.

5. Mills had always intended to return to his hobo notes. A letter from his father, Robert Alexander Mills, on March 3, 1940, mentions this interest. After his heart attack in 1953, Mills was forced to reduce his professional commitments, and he turned to his long-delayed project. In a letter to Dudley Cates dated April 2, 1953, Mills wrote that "your little expedition into the past in your fragment of history has turned my thoughts back to the pre-1914 era. As you may remember, I did some hoboing with Carleton Parker, joining the IWW in the process, and studying the aftermath of the Wheatland riot. I kept notes while I was on the road, and it has always been my hope that I could work these up sometime into some sort of an account of migratory and hobo life in that period. I have turned back to these notes recently and if time permits and stimulation persists, I should like to add another fragment or two to your contribution." Mills's papers also include correspondence with the National Archives in 1955 in search of material for his project.

6. Mills, draft of untitled novel, Mills papers, 25–33. The IWW was particularly active in denouncing the employment agency game. The first major IWW free speech fight in Spokane, Washington, in 1909 began over the exploitative practices of private employment agencies. See Dubofsky, *We Shall Be All,* 175–76; and Kornbluh, *Rebel Voices,* 68, 80. Itinerants were exploited by other schemes as well. Wyckoff described how the unemployed

in Chicago were cheated by ads for people to color photographs. Although promised high wages, employees soon found they could barely make enough to pay the fees charged for supplies. Wyckoff, *The Workers: An Experiment in Reality,* vol. 2, *The West,* 121–22.

7. Mills, "Sand Creek," 8.

8. The early 1900s marked the beginning of modern analysis of unemployment. Through the late 1800s the dominant view had been that unemployment was a matter of personal responsibility. This may have been an adequate position in an agricultural economy, but it had little relevance in industrial economies with recurring business cycles. A turning point in the history of analysis of unemployment came with the publication of William Beveridge's *Unemployment: A Problem of Industry* in 1909. Beveridge's position was precisely what his title indicated—that unemployment was due to industrial malfunctions rather than to personal failings. The development of a system of public labor exchanges was an important part of Beveridge's policy recommendations. By 1914, active discussions about the "new views" of unemployment had led to significant reforms in Europe but had enjoyed little legislative impact in the United States. It was not until the Great Depression that the United States finally gave up its policy allegiance to the "individual responsibility" theory of unemployment. The importance of Beveridge's book in influencing the recommendations of the California CIH is shown by the fact that the CIH *Report on Unemployment* of December 1914 gave it first place and the most space in appendix B-2, a "Digest of Several Books on Unemployment." The history of economic and policy thought about unemployment is covered in John A. Garraty, *Unemployment in History.* For a recent discussion of the debate in Mills's time over public employment agencies, see Udo Sautter, "North American Government Labor Agencies before World War One: A Cure for Unemployment?"

9. California CIH, *Report on Unemployment,* 6–7, 12. Mills, "Sand Creek," 8.

10. Leiserson, "Labor Market," 14, 24.

11. Ibid., 75–76.

12. Mills, "The Hobo," BB.

13. Ibid., BB-CC.

Chapter 5. Walking the Roads

1. Mills, "The Ritual of the Road."

2. McCook, "Leaves from the Diary of a Tramp," Dec. 5, 1901; London, *The Road;* Wyckoff, *The Workers: An Experiment in Reality,* vol. 1, *The East,* 54–55, 80–81, 90–91. Mills's descriptions of hobo life are consistent with recent hobo histories by Bruns, *Knights of the Road;* Allsop, *Hard Travellin';* and Monkkonen, ed., *Walking to Work.*

3. Michael Mathers, *Riding the Rails,* and Harper, *Good Company.* See Harper, pp. 148–49, for a discussion of the distinct periods of hobo history. Also Kusmer, "The Underclass." The argument that migrants of the 1930s

were refugees is presented in Bruns, *Knights of the Road*, 190. Harper's discussion of the last niches for the hobo worker is on pp. 150–51.

4. Mathers's comparison of today's jungles to those in the past is in Mathers, *Riding the Rails*, 60–70. On p. 54 Mathers discusses the derelict proportion of the current hobo population and estimates that "alcohol was a necessary traveling companion to sixty percent of the men on the road." Also see Monkkonen, Introduction, 2–3. The rules of jungle life in Mills's time are discussed in Kornbluh, *Rebel Voices*, 67; and Anderson, *The Hobo*, 20–21.

5. Mills, "Jungles," 1.

6. London's discussion of "gay-cats" versus "road-kids" is in London, *The Road*, 333.

7. The following accounts are from Mills, "Scenes and Incidents 'On the Road,' " 1–11.

8. Mills's correspondence in November 1955 with the National Archives is included in his papers.

Chapter 6. Riding the Rails

1. London, *The Road*.

2. See Bruns, *Knights of the Road*, 46, for the ICC data. Also see Kornbluh, *Rebel Voices*, 66, for other data on the number of men killed and injured stealing rides on trains. McCook, "Leaves from the Diary of a Tramp," December 5, 1901, contains photographs of various ways to ride trains. McCook's photographs are included in the papers of John J. McCook at the Antiquarian and Landmarks Society of Hartford, Connecticut.

3. The practice by unions of issuing traveling cards for identification purposes is discussed by Patricia A. Cooper, "The 'Traveling Fraternity': Union Cigar Makers and Geographic Mobility, 1900–1919," in *Walking to Work*, 125–26; and by Jules Tygiel, "Tramping Artisans: Carpenters in Industrial America, 1880–90," in *Walking to Work*, 104–5. For the practice of allowing tramps free rides, see Monkkonen, Introduction, 10–11.

4. Mills, "Record," Marysville, July 17, 1914.

Chapter 7. Observing the IWW

1. The history of the IWW in California is covered in Brissenden, *The IWW*; Dubofsky, *We Shall Be All*; Weintraub, "The I.W.W. in California"; Wilson, "The I.W.W. in California"; and Daniel, *Bitter Harvest*. Dubofsky has the best presentation of the activities of the IWW outside of California.

2. Dubofsky, *We Shall Be All*, 152–65, discusses the IWW philosophy in detail. The strikes at Paterson and Lawrence are covered in chapters 10 and 11 of this work.

3. The Fresno and San Diego free speech fights are covered in Dubofsky, *We Shall Be All*, 185–96. For the Wheatland incident and its aftermath, see

Dubofsky, *We Shall Be All*, 294–300, and Daniel, *Bitter Harvest*, 84–99. Philip S. Foner argues that the short-term "result of the Wheatland affair was an increase in I.W.W. prestige and membership." *History of the Labor Movement in the United States*, 4:278–80. Daniel argues that the long-term consequence of Wheatland was to reduce the effectiveness of the IWW by "fixing in the public's mind an image of the IWW that hardly enhanced its reputation as a labor union and surely facilitated the work of those who lobbied for federal suppression of the organization in 1917." *Bitter Harvest*, 86. Since at the time Mills took his trip the IWW had only been active in rural districts of California for five years, it was reasonable to expect that the union's rapid rise would continue. Mills was not alone in suggesting that the IWW could create severe disturbances in the near future. Speek, "Report on the Interviews with Unemployed Migratory Workers in San Francisco," 3–4, and Brissenden, "A Report on the I.W.W. in California," 14–15, voiced similar fears. It is only with hindsight that we know that the IWW shortly would be eliminated as a major influence among California's itinerant laborers.

4. Mills, "Scenes and Incidents 'On the Road,' " 15–16.

5. Controversy over the Ford-Suhr trial was illustrated in testimony before the Commission on Industrial Relations in San Francisco in August 1914. See the testimony of George Bell, W. H. Carlin, A. B. McKenzie, Austin Lewis, Robert M. Royce, William Mundell, and Edward B. Stanwood in the U.S. Commission on Industrial Relations, *Final Report*, 5:4979–5026. For photographs of workers demonstrating in Wheatland in August 1914, see Street, " 'We Are Not Slaves.' "

6. Mills, "Orange Industry," 9.

7. Mills, "Survey of Lumber Camp," 10–11.

8. Support for the IWW among the unskilled and disenfranchised is emphasized by most writers on the IWW. See Dubofsky, *We Shall Be All*, 291–93; Robert L. Tyler, *Rebels of the Woods: The I.W.W. in the Pacific Northwest*, 9–10; and Kornbluh, *Rebel Voices*, 66–67. The limits of the impact of the IWW during the time when Mills was traveling are also discussed by Daniel, *Bitter Harvest*, 86.

9. Mills, "The Hobo," AA.

10. Mills's conclusions about the hardships of itinerant life are supported in contemporary reports by investigators in other parts of the country. See Duffus, "Labor Market Conditions"; Speek, "Report on Psychological Aspect of the Problem of Floating Laborers," and "Preliminary Investigation of the Harvest Hand Situation." Speek summarized his findings in "The Psychology of Floating Workers."

11. Brissenden, "Report on the I.W.W.," 15. Speek, "Report on the Interviews with Unemployed Migratory Workers," 3–4. Parker, "The I.W.W.," *Atlantic Monthly*, November 1917, reprinted in Parker, *Casual Laborer*, 123, 107.

12. Parker asked Mills to check on rumors about a hop fields strike. Mills's visits to IWW halls were part of this investigation. See the letter from Parker

to Simon Lubin of the CIH, July 7, 1914, Lubin Collection, Bancroft Library. Mills's IWW card is included in his personal papers.

13. Carleton H. Parker was an outspoken critic of the IWW. Brissenden was a fellow Immigration Commission investigator.

14. MacNamara was not one of the McNamara brothers who dynamited the *Los Angeles Times* building. The McNamara brothers were in jail at the time. See Adamic, *Dynamite*, 242.

15. Mills, "Case 1-," d-e. The "dangerous discontent" Mills experienced was affirmed by Peter A. Speek in his visit to San Francisco in October 1914. See Speek, "Report on the Interviews with Unemployed Migratory Workers."

16. Mills, "Case 1-," e-f. Kornbluh, *Rebel Voices*, 71, discusses the history of the song "Hallelujah on the Bum." Most of the famous IWW songs are included in Kornbluh's book.

Chapter 8. Conclusions

1. McWilliams, *Factories in the Field*, 166–67.

2. The achievements of the CIH are discussed in its *Annual Reports*. Also see Wood, "California State Commission of Immigration and Housing."

3. The fact that Mills did not keep records of his last months with the CIH suggests his evaluation of the importance of his various assignments. Mills's later duties are summarized in a letter of recommendation written by CIH attorney George Bell.

4. The reference to Mills coming down with malaria is in Cornelia Stratton Parker, *Idyll*, 83. A draft exists in Mills's papers of the section "Data Gathered 'On the Road' " in Parker, "Preliminary Report on Migratory Labor in California," submitted to the CIR in September 1914. Mills also wrote the analyses of the orange and lumber industries in the section of the same report entitled "Labor Markets in Certain Sectors and Industries."

5. The CIR hearings in San Francisco are in CIR, *Final Report*, 5:4911–5027. Parker's professional work is discussed in detail in Cornelia Stratton Parker, *Idyll*.

6. For a record of the actions of the CIH in 1914, see the *Annual Report* for that year (issued in January 1915) and the CIH *Report on Unemployment* (issued in December 1914). Various interpretations of the issues behind Parker's resignation are presented in Cornelia Stratton Parker, *Idyll*, 88, and Daniel, *Bitter Harvest*, 99. Also see letters related to the resignation: Lubin to Parker (September 30, 1914), Parker to Lubin (October 3, 1914), Lubin to Cornelia Stratton Parker (October 10, 1914), and Cornelia Stratton Parker to Lubin (October 14, 1914) in the Lubin Collection.

7. Mills's disavowal of being an "undercover agent" is in a letter dated August 7, 1955, in Mills's papers (chap. 2, n. 2). Mills's sympathy with the plight of itinerant laborers is discussed in Speek, "Notes on the Situation of Migratory Laborers and Unemployment in California." Later writers about the CIH at times have assumed incorrectly that CIH investigators were spies

from the very beginning. See Daniel, *Bitter Harvest*, 98–99; and Elizabeth Reis, "Cannery Row: The AFL, the IWW and Bay Area Italian Cannery Workers," 188. The labor espionage activities of the CIH are discussed in detail in Reis, "Cannery Row," 188–90; Wood, "California State Commission of Immigration and Housing," 263–72; and Nelson, "J. Vance Thompson."

8. For the outcome of the CIR's investigations, see Adams, *Age of Industrial Violence*, chap. 10; and Dubofsky, "Abortive Reform," 204–6.

9. The repression of the IWW is discussed in all histories of the organization. For a thorough presentation, see Dubofsky, *We Shall Be All*, 349–444.

10. For arguments that the large numbers of men on the road in Mills's day were a consequence of the evolution of the United States from an agricultural to an industrial and service economy see Anderson, *The Hobo*, xviii-xx; Kusmer, "The Underclass," 21–22; and Monkkonen, Introduction, 2–3.

11. Mills, untitled novel, 118–20.

12. Mills, untitled novel, 314–19. For an overview of the actions of The Commonwealth Club see "Handling Unemployment in California," *the Survey*, and "Unemployment," *Transactions of the Commonwealth Club of California*.

Bibliography

All letters cited in this book are either in Frederick C. Mills's papers, which are held by his son William H. Mills, or in the Simon Lubin Collection, Bancroft Library, University of California, Berkeley.

Adamic, Louis. *Dynamite: The Story of Class Violence in America.* New York: Viking Press, 1931.

Adams, Charles E. "The Real Hobo: What He Is and How He Lives." *Forum* 33 (June 1902): 438–39.

Adams, Graham, Jr. *Age of Industrial Violence, 1910–15: The Activities and Findings of the United States Commission on Industrial Relations.* New York: Columbia University Press, 1966.

Adams, R. L. and T. R. Kelly. *A Study of Farm Labor in California.* Berkeley: University of California, College of Agriculture, Berkeley Agricultural Experiment Station, March 1918.

Allsop, Kenneth. *Hard Travellin': The Hobo and His History.* New York: New American Library, 1967.

Anderson, Nels. *The Hobo.* Chicago: University of Chicago Press, 1961.

Andrews, Ralph W. *Redwood Classic.* New York: Bonanza Books, 1968.

Baily, Samuel. "The Adjustment of Italian Immigrants in Buenos Aires and New York, 1870–1914." *American Historical Review* 88 (April 1983): 281–305.

Beveridge, William. *Unemployment: A Problem of Industry.* London: Longmans, Green and Co., 1909.

Brissenden, Paul. "A Report on the I.W.W. in California," August 1914. Typescript. U.S. Commission on Industrial Relations, Department of Labor, Record Group 174, National Archives, Washington, D.C.

———. *The I.W.W.: A Study of American Syndicalism.* New York: Columbia University Press, 1919.

Bruns, Roger. *Knights of the Road: A Hobo History.* New York: Methuen, 1980.

Bye, Raymond T. *Critiques of Research in the Social Sciences, II: An Appraisal of Frederick C. Mills' The Behavior of Prices.* New York: Social Science Research Council, 1940.

California. Commission of Immigration and Housing. *Report on Unemployment.* Sacramento: GPO, December 9, 1914.

———. *First Annual Report of the Commission of Immigration and Housing of California.* Sacramento: GPO, 1915.

Cooper, Patricia A. "The 'Traveling Fraternity': Union Cigar Makers and Geographic Mobility, 1900–1919." In *Walking to Work: Tramps in America: 1790–1935*, edited by Eric H. Monkkonen, 118–38. Lincoln: University of Nebraska Press, 1984.

"Correspondence Relative to Wheatland Riot Trials Held at Marysville, California, January 1914." Typescript. U.S. Commission on Industrial Relations, Department of Labor, Record Group 174, National Archives, Washington, D.C.

Daniel, Cletus. *Bitter Harvest: A History of California Farmworkers, 1870–1941*. Ithaca, N.Y.: Cornell University Press, 1981.

Dubofsky, Melvin. *We Shall Be All: A History of the Industrial Workers of the World*. Chicago: Quadrangle Books, 1969.

———. "Abortive Reform: The Wilson Administration and Organized Labor, 1913–1920." In *Work, Community, and Power: The Experience of Labor in Europe and America, 1900–1925*, edited by James E. Cronin and Carmen Sirianni, 197–220. Philadelphia: Temple University Press, 1983.

Duffus, William. "Labor Market Conditions in the Harvest Fields of the Middle West." December 1, 1914. Typescript. U.S. Commission on Industrial Relations, Department of Labor, Record Group 174, National Archives, Washington, D.C.

Edwards, Richard C., Michael Reich, and David M. Gordon, eds. *Labor Market Segmentation*. Lexington, Mass.: Heath, 1975.

Ficken, Robert E. "The Wobbly Horrors: Pacific Northwest Lumbermen and the Industrial Workers of the World, 1917–1918." *Labor History* 24 (Summer 1983): 325–41.

Fisher, Lloyd. *The Harvest Labor Market in California*. Cambridge: Harvard University Press, 1953.

Fitch, John A. "Old and New Labor Problems in California." *Survey* 32 (September 19, 1914): 608–10.

Flynt, Josiah. *Tramping With Tramps: Studies and Sketches of Vagabond Life*. New York: The Century Co., 1901.

Foner, Philip S. *History of the Labor Movement in the United States*. Vol. 4. New York: International Publishers, 1965.

Forbes, James. "The Tramp; or, Caste in the Jungle." *Outlook* 98 (August 19, 1911): 869–75.

Fuller, Vardon. "The Supply of Agricultural Labor as a Factor in the Evolution of Farm Organization in California." U.S. Congress. Senate. Subcommittee of the Committee on Education and Labor. *Violations of Free Speech and Rights of Labor*. 76th Cong. 3d Sess., 1940. Pt. 54.

Garraty, John A. *Unemployment in History*. New York: Harper and Row, 1978.

Graham, Hugh Davis, and Ted Robert Gurr, eds. *The History of Violence in America: Historical and Comparative Perspectives*. New York: Praeger, 1969.

Grosse, Marion A. "A Century of Lumbering in Fresno County." In *Fresno County Centennial Almanac*. Fresno, California: Fresno County Centennial Committee, April 1956.

Gutman, Herbert G. "Work, Culture, and Society in Industrializing America, 1815–1919." *American Historical Review* 78 (June 1973): 531–88.

"Handling Unemployment in California." *The Survey* 33 (August 1915): 483.

Harper, Douglas. *Good Company*. Chicago: University of Chicago Press, 1982.

Hofstadter, Richard, and Michael Wallace, eds. *American Violence: A Documentary History*. New York: Knopf, 1970.

Hunter, Robert. *Poverty*. New York: MacMillan Co., 1904.

Katz, Michael B. *Poverty and Policy in American History*. New York: Academic Press, 1983.

Keyssar, Alexander. *Out of Work: The First Century of Unemployment in Massachusetts*. Cambridge: University of Cambridge Press, 1986.

Klein, Herbert S. "The Integration of Italian Immigrants into the United States and Argentina: A Comparative Analysis." *American Historical Review* 88 (April 1983): 306–29.

Kornbluh, Joyce L. *Rebel Voices: An I.W.W. Anthology*. Ann Arbor: University of Michigan Press, 1964.

Kusmer, Kenneth L. "The Underclass in Historical Perspective: Tramps and Vagrants in Urban America, 1870–1930." In *On Being Homeless: Historical Perspectives*, edited by Rick Beard, 21–31. New York: Museum of the City of New York, 1987.

Lauck, W. Jett, and Edgar Sydenstricker. *Conditions of Labor in American Industries: A Summarization of the Results of Recent Investigations*. New York: Funk and Wagnalls Company, 1917.

Leiserson, William. "The Labor Market and Unemployment." February 15, 1915. Typescript. U.S. Commission on Industrial Relations, Department of Labor, Record Group 174, National Archives, Washington, D.C.

Lens, Sidney. *The Labor Wars: From the Molly Maguires to the Sitdowns*. New York: Doubleday, 1973.

Loftis, Anne, and Dick Meister. *A Long Time Coming: The Struggle to Unionize America's Farm Workers*. New York: MacMillan, 1977.

London, Jack. *The Bodley Head Jack London*. Edited by Arthur Calder-Marshall. Vol. 2, *The Road*. London: Bodley Head, 1964.

McCook, John J. "Leaves from the Diary of a Tramp." *Independent* 53 (November 21, 1901): 2760–67; (December 5, 1901): 2880–88; (December 19, 1901): 3009–13; 54 (January 2, 1902): 23–28; (January 16, 1902): 154–60; (February 6, 1902): 332–37; (April 10, 1902): 873–74; (June 6, 1902): 1539–44.

McGee, Lizzie. *Mills of the Sequoias*. Visalia, California: Tulare County Historical Society, 1952.

McGowan, Joseph A. *History of the Sacramento Valley*. Vol. 2. New York: Lewis Historical Publishing Company, 1961.

McWilliams, Carey. *Factories in the Field: The Story of Migratory Farm Labor in California*. Boston: Little, Brown, 1939.

Majka, Linda, and Theo Majka. *Farm Workers, Agribusiness and the State*. Philadelphia: Temple University Press, 1982.

Mathers, Michael. *Riding the Rails*. Boston: Gambit, 1973.

Mills, Frederick C. "Case 1-." 1914. Typescript. Mills papers.

————. "E-6." 1914. Typescript. Mills papers.

————. "An Economic Survey of a Sierra Lumber Camp." 1914. Typescript. Mills papers.

————. "The Hobo and the Migratory Casual on the Road." 1914. Typescript. Mills papers.

————. "Jungles." 1914. Typescript. Mills papers.

————. "The Orange Industry of Central California." 1914. Typescript. Mills papers.

————. "Record." 1914. Typescript. Mills papers.

————. "The Ritual of the Road." 1914. Typescript. Mills papers.

————. "The Sand Creek Road Situation." 1914. Typescript. Mills papers.

————. "Scenes and Incidents 'On the Road.' " 1914. Typescript. Mills papers.

————. "A Supplementary Report Concerning Orange Picking Conditions." 1914. Typescript. Mills papers.

————. *Contemporary Theories of Unemployment and of Unemployment Relief*. New York: Columbia University Press, 1917.

————. "On Measurement in Economics." *The Trend of Economics*. Edited by Rexford Guy Tugwell. New York: Alfred A. Knopf, 1924: 37–70.

————. *The Behavior of Prices*. New York: The National Bureau of Economic Research, 1927.

————. "Of Friday and Edie and Ayres." *Journal of the American Statistical Association* 32 (December 1937): 4–5.

————. Autobiographical statement, May 12, 1942. Typescript. Mills papers.

————. Draft of untitled novel. 1953 (?). Typescript. Mills papers.

Monkkonen, Eric H. Introduction to *Walking to Work: Tramps in America, 1790–1935*, edited by Eric H. Monkkonen, 1–17. Lincoln: University of Nebraska Press, 1984.

————, ed. *Walking to Work: Tramps in America: 1790–1935*. Lincoln: University of Nebraska Press, 1984.

Montgomery, David. *Workers' Control in America: Studies in the History of Work, Technology, and Labor Struggles*. Cambridge: Cambridge University Press, 1979.

————. *The Fall of the House of Labor: The Workplace, the State, and American Labor Activism, 1865–1925*. Cambridge: Cambridge University Press, 1987.

Moses, Vincent. "Oranges for Health—California for Wealth: The Billion-Dollar Navel and the California Dream." *The Californians* 3 (July/August 1985): 27–37.

Mowry, George E. *The California Progressives*. Chicago: Quadrangle, 1951.

Nelson, Bruce. "J. Vance Thompson, the Industrial Workers of the World, and the Mood of Syndicalism, 1914–1921." *Labor's Heritage* 2 (October 1990): 45–65.

Parker, Carleton H. "The Wheatland Riot and What Lay Back of It." *The Survey* 31 (March 21, 1914): 768–70.

———. *Report on the Wheatland Hop-Fields Riot.* March 30, 1914. Typescript. U.S. Commission on Industrial Relations, Department of Labor, Record Group 174, National Archives, Washington, D.C.

———. "Unemployment and the Migratory Worker." June 17, 1914. Typescript. U.S. Commission on Industrial Relations, Department of Labor, Record Group 174, National Archives, Washington, D.C.

———. "Preliminary Report on Tentative Findings and Conclusions in the Investigation of Seasonal, Migratory and Unskilled Labor in California." September 1, 1914. Typescript. U.S. Commission on Industrial Relations, Department of Labor, Record Group 174, National Archives, Washington, D.C.

———. "The California Casual and His Revolt." *Quarterly Journal of Economics* 30 (November 1915): 110–26.

———. *The Casual Laborer and Other Essays.* New York: Harcourt, Brace and Howe, 1920.

———. "A Report on Employment Agencies in California." N.d. Typescript. U.S. Commission on Industrial Relations, Department of Labor, Record Group 174, National Archives, Washington, D.C.

Parker, Cornelia Stratton. *An American Idyll: The Life of Carleton H. Parker.* Boston: Atlantic Monthly, 1919.

Piore, Michael J. *Birds of Passage: Migrant Labor and Industrial Societies.* Cambridge: Cambridge University Press, 1979.

Reis, Elizabeth. "Cannery Row: The AFL, the IWW and Bay Area Italian Cannery Workers." *California History* 64 (Summer 1985): 174–91.

Riis, Jacob A. *How the Other Half Lives: Studies Among the Tenements of New York.* 1890; New York: Hill and Wang, 1957.

Robinson, William Wilcox. *The Story of Tulare County and Visalia.* 2d ed. Los Angeles: Title Insurance and Trust Co., 1964.

Rodgers, Daniel T. *The Work Ethic in Industrializing America, 1850–1920.* Chicago: University of Chicago Press, 1978.

Roske, Ralph J. *Everyman's Eden: A History of California.* New York: Macmillan, 1968.

Rubenstein, Richard E. *Rebels in Eden: Mass Political Violence in the United States.* Boston: Little, Brown, 1970.

Sautter, Udo. "North American Government Labor Agencies before World War One: A Cure for Unemployment?" *Labor History* 24 (Summer 1983): 366–93.

Schneider, John C. "Tramping Workers, 1890–1920: A Subcultural View." In *Walking to Work,* edited by Eric H. Monkkonen, 212–34.

Selvin, David F. *Sky Full of Storm: A Brief History of California Labor,* rev. ed. San Francisco: California Historical Society, 1975.

Sloan, Irving J. *Our Violent Past: An American Chronicle*. New York: Random House, 1970.

Speek, Peter A. "Report on the Preliminary Investigation of the Harvest Hand Situation in the States of Kansas and Missouri." July 30, 1914. Typescript. U.S. Commission on Industrial Relations, Department of Labor, Record Group 174, National Archives, Washington, D.C.

———. "Notes on the Situation of Migratory Laborers and Unemployment in California." October 3, 1914. Typescript. U.S. Commission on Industrial Relations, Department of Labor, Record Group 174, National Archives, Washington, D.C.

———. "Report on the Interviews with Unemployed Migratory Workers in the Streets and Public Parks in San Francisco." October 14, 1914. Typescript. U.S. Commission on Industrial Relations, Department of Labor, Record Group 174, National Archives, Washington, D.C.

———. "Report on Psychological Aspect of the Problem of Floating Laborers: An Analysis of Life Stories." June 25, 1915. Typescript. U.S. Commission on Industrial Relations, Department of Labor, Record Group 174, National Archives, Washington, D.C.

———. "The Psychology of Floating Workers." *Annals of the American Academy of Political and Social Science* 69 (January 1917): 72–78.

Steinbeck, John. *The Grapes of Wrath*. New York: Viking Press, 1939.

Street, Richard S. "'We Are Not Slaves': The Photographic Record of the Wheatland Hop Riot; First Photographs of Protesting Farm Workers in America." *Southern California Quarterly* 64 (Fall 1982): 205–26.

Talbott, E. Guy. "The Armies of the Unemployed in California." *The Survey* 32 (August 22, 1914): 523–24.

Tilly, Charles, Louise Tilly, and Richard Tilly. *The Rebellious Century: 1830–1930*. Cambridge, Mass.: Harvard University Press, 1975.

Tygiel, Jules. "Tramping Artisans: Carpenters in Industrial America, 1880–90." In *Walking to Work*, edited by Eric H. Monkkonen, 87–117.

Tyler, Robert L. *Rebels of the Woods: The I.W.W. in the Pacific Northwest*. Eugene: University of Oregon Press, 1967.

"Unemployment." *Transactions of the Commonwealth Club of California* 9 (December 1914): 671–714.

United States. Commission on Industrial Relations. *Final Report and Testimony Submitted to Congress by the Commission on Industrial Relations*. Vol. 5. Washington, D.C.: GPO, 1916.

United States. Department of Commerce. *Statistical Abstract of the United States: 1916*. Washington, D.C.: GPO, 1917.

Waters, Theodore. "Six Weeks in Beggardom." *Everybody's Magazine* 11 (1904): 789–97; 12 (1905): 69–78.

Weintraub, Hyman. "The I.W.W. in California, 1905–1931." M.A. thesis, University of California, Los Angeles, 1947.

Whitten, Woodrow C. "The Wheatland Episode." *Pacific Historical Review* 17 (February 1948): 37–42.

Williams, Richard L. *The Loggers*. New York: Time-Life Books, 1976.

Wilson, Ione E. "The I.W.W. in California with Special Reference to Migratory Labor." M.A. thesis, University of California, Berkeley, 1946.
Wood, Samuel Edgerton. "The California State Commission of Immigration and Housing: A Study of Administrative Organization and the Growth of Function." Ph.D. diss., University of California, Berkeley, 1942.
Wyckoff, Walter. *The Workers: An Experiment in Reality.* 2 vols. New York: Charles Scribner's Sons, 1897.

Index

Adams, Graham, Jr.: on labor violence, 10
Agriculture: need for labor, 6; organization of, 17; workers in, after Mills's trip, 134. *See also* Mills, Frederick C.
American Economic Association: and Mills, 16
American Federation of Labor: in contrast to IWW, 115, 125
American Friends Service Committee: and Mills, 15, 144n14
American Statistical Association: and Mills, 14, 16
Anderson, California: and railroads, 111
Auburn, California: and railroads, 104

Ball (road contractor): and employment agency game, 65, 66, 72, 93; camp of, 66, 69–72. *See also* Mills, Frederick C.
Ben (character in Mills's novel), 135; on employment agency game, 68–72
Berkeley, California: employment agencies in, 67. *See also* Mills, Frederick C.: background
Biggs, California: and railroads, 106, 108
Black workers. *See* Workers
Brighton Junction, California, 121; and railroads, 104
Brissenden, Paul, 126; hired by Immigration Commission, 22; on the IWW, 121–22

California: history of agricultural labor in, 6, 9; interest by, in labor issues, 10–11; as state of summer employment, 20–21; seasonality of manufacturing employment in, 21; lumber industry in, 42; dual labor

market in, 62, 63; employment agencies in, 66–68. *See also* Agriculture; Employment agencies; Industrial Workers of the World; Lumber industry; Mills, Frederick C.; Orange industry; Road Construction
California Commission of Immigration and Housing (CIH), 66, 135. *See also* Paul Brissenden
—activities during World War I, 131, 133
—headquarters of, 20, 22, 108, 131
—and labor: on public employment agencies, 72–73; and the IWW, 133; move toward labor espionage, 133, 145n2, 152n7
—mandate, 10, 11
—as Mills's employer, 1, 13, 131; trips to Lindsay and Hume, 22–23, 41, 146n3
—Mills's reports for, x, 95; on Hume lumber camp, 42, 45, 57–58, 59, 60, 61–63, 64; on Sand Creek Road, 65, 66, 72, 73; on "the road," 88
—policy recommendations of, 137
—programs, 11, 64, 131
—reports, 11, 12; on unemployment, 11, 12, 72–73, 132
—and resignation of Carleton H. Parker, 132–33
California Express (train), 105
Casual workers. *See* Itinerant workers
Central Valley of California: as location of Mills's trip, 1, 3, 20, 42, 77, 78, 82, 95, 97, 132; description of, 17; economic development of, 17; IWW in, 122
Chicago, Illinois, 93, 117; and the IWW, 115
Chico, California: and railroads, 104, 108, 109

CIH. *See* California Commission of Immigration and Housing
Citrus Cove, California: Mills in, 87
CIR. *See* United States Commission on Industrial Relations
Columbia University. *See* Mills, Frederick C.: background
Commission of Immigration and Housing. *See* California Commission of Immigration and Housing
Commonwealth Club of California: and unemployment, 137, 140
Connellan (IWW local leader): and Mills, 124, 126
Cottonwood, California: and railroads, 111

Dad's Hotel, Lindsay, California, 31, 32, 34
Devlin, Dare-Devil (IWW speaker): and Mills, 124, 126
Dinuba, California, 41, 69, 117; Mills in, 84–85; itinerants at water tank in, 88–90
Donkey engines: at Hume, 45, 47, 52; disappearance of, 134
Downing (IWW speaker), 126
Drake orange packinghouse, 31, 33; and hiring of Mills, 24–25; working conditions, 25; role of "rustlers," 26, 28; workers, 26, 29–30; women employees, 29. *See also* Mills, Frederick C.
Dunlap, California, 41, 54; Mills in, 87
Durst, Ralph (hop ranch owner): 5, 9; comments on, by itinerants, 117, 118, 123. *See also* Durst hop ranch
Durst hop ranch: labor camp at, 5; and job ads, 5, 24; and Wheatland riot, 5–6. *See also* Wheatland riot

Econometric Society: and Mills, 16
Edwards (IWW speaker), 126
Employment agencies: Immigration Commission on, 11, 72; in California, 49, 66, 67–68, 70, 71; nationwide practices of, 68; U.S. Commission on Industrial Relations on, 72; as cure for unemployment, 72–75; in Europe, 73

Employment agency game: illegality of, 66, 67, 68; Mills on, 66, 68, 72; description of, 66, 70; evidence of, 67
Eugene, Oregon: and railroads, 114
Exeter, California, 23

Fitch, John A.: on California seasonal work, 20
Flynt, Josiah: on hobo life, 1–2
Ford, Richard "Blackie" (IWW leader): at Wheatland, 6; itinerants' comments on, 117, 118, 123, 126
Fresno, California, 30, 69, 83, 85, 94; as start of Mills's trip, 1, 23; and employment agencies, 66, 68, 70, 71; and railroads, 99, 101, 102, 105; and the IWW, 116, 122

Galt, California: and railroads, 108
George's Place, Lindsay, California, 33, 35
Gridley, California: and railroads, 108
Groller (character in Mills's novel): on itinerant labor, 135–37

Harper, Douglas: on recent hobo life, 77–78; on number of itinerant workers since 1860, 78
Hindu workers. *See* Workers: Asian Indian
Hinman House, Lindsay, California, 32
Hoboes. *See* Itinerant workers
Hobo jungles. *See* Jungles
Hooker, California: and railroads, 111
Hume, California, 65, 82, 85–88, 93; lumber industry around, 41–63 passim. *See also* Mills, Frederick C.
Hume-Bennett Lumber Company: history of, 42, 43. *See also* Mills, Frederick C.

Immigration and Housing Commission. *See* California Commission of Immigration and Housing
Immigration Commission. *See* California Commission of Immigration and Housing
Industrial Relations Commission. *See* United States Commission on Industrial Relations

Industrial Workers of the World (IWW), 20, 28, 104, 108, 135; and Wheatland riot, 5–6, 116; songs, 6, 124, 126, 129–30; Carleton Parker on, 11; and the Immigration Commission, 12, 133; Mills's membership in, 14, 124; history and philosophy of, 115; in California (1905–13), 115, 116; itinerants' comments on, 116–22 passim; free speech fights of, 116, 124; supporters and critics of, 117–19, 120, 127–28; investigators' comments on, 121–22; description of locals, 124–27; opposition to World War I, 134; suppression by government, 134. *See also* American Federation of Labor; Mills, Frederick C.

Itinerant workers
—attitudes of: toward work, 26, 30, 53, 54, 59, 88–89, 91–92, 93, 94, 95, 119–20; and humor among, 30, 56, 92, 103–4, 112–14, 129–30; toward bosses, 30, 71; toward the law, 35, 89, 90, 95
—characteristics of: distinctive vocabulary, 1, 56, 67, 76–77, 82, 104, 112–13, 130; marital status, 5, 26, 37–39, 50, 51, 53–54, 59, 125, 128, 136–37; types on the road, 21, 55, 57–58, 78, 81–82, 92, 95, 100–101; style of eating, 33, 57, 79, 106; age of men on the road, 53, 60, 88, 90, 91, 94
—problems of: pressure to degenerate, 3, 38–39, 61–62, 74–75, 90, 94, 101; unemployment, 9, 137, 138; decline in twentieth century, 78, 134–35; unrest among, 120–21, 127–28
—social problem of: 2–3, 6; early investigators of, 1–2; lack of sympathy toward, 2, 6, 9, 11; lack of information about, 2–3, 9, 10, 11, 135, 136–37, 140; Carleton Parker on, 11; and importance of accurate observations, 75, 95, 135–37, 140; indecisive policy debates about, 133–34, 137–40. *See also* California; Industrial Workers of the World; Job

advertising practices; Jungles; Mills, Frederick C.

IWW. *See* Industrial Workers of the World

Job advertising practices: at Durst hop ranch, 5, 24; in Lindsay, 22, 24; in the Midwest, 24; in *The Grapes of Wrath*, 24

Johnson, Hiram (governor of California), 6, 10–11, 133

Jones, Smoky (IWW speaker): and Mills, 124–25, 126

Jungles: as center of hobo life, 78, 80; meals at, 79; stories told in, 81; relation to railroads, 97; and the IWW, 116. *See also* Marysville, California; Mills, Frederick C.

Kelley's Army, 131; story of, 9; as incentive to investigate itinerancy, 10; California Immigration Commission report on, 12

King's River, California, 44, 85

Labor violence, 10, 128

Lauck, W. Jett: on pre–World War I itinerancy, 2; on California seasonal work, 20

Leiserson, William H.: on private employment agencies, 68; on public employment agencies, 73, 74

Lindsay, California, 21, 22, 34, 37, 39, 41, 49, 68, 82, 88, 89, 101; description of area around, 23, 32, 33, 82–83; lodging and meals at, 26, 31–35 passim; and the IWW, 119. *See also* Drake orange packinghouse

Live Oak, California: and railroads, 105, 106, 108

London, Jack, 2, 128; on hobo life, 77; on gay-cats and road-kids, 82

Los Angeles, California: unemployment in, 9; employment agencies in, 49, 67

Lumber industry: near Hume, California, 42–63 passim; workers compared to orange workers, 55, 63; labor turnover in, 58; after Mills's trip, 64, 134; workers and the IWW, 119–20. *See also* Hume-Bennett

Lumber Company; Mills, Frederick
C.

McCook, John J.: on hobo life, 1; hobo
photos by, 77
MacNamara (IWW agent): and Mills,
127
McWilliams, Carey: on itinerant issues,
131
Marysville, California, 81, 104, 113,
118, 119; jungles in, 78–80, 106;
and railroads, 105, 106, 108
Mathers, Michael: on recent hobo life,
77–78
Migrant workers. See Itinerant workers
Mills, Frederick C. See also Parker,
Carleton H.; Parker, Cornelia Stratton
—background: Columbia University, ix,
16, 17, 132; personal, 12, 14, 15, 16,
132; professional memberships, 14,
16; University of California at
Berkeley, 14, 16, 20, 23, 53, 132;
military service, 14, 132; professional
accomplishments, 15, 16, 132,
144n16; strength of convictions, 15,
144n14; retirement and death, 17
—hobo papers, ix–x, 1; draft of novel
among, x, 1, 68, 135, 148n5;
sympathy toward itinerants in, 2,
142n4; and National Archives, 95,
148n5
—hobo trip: itinerary, 1, 17, 20, 41, 82;
pseudonym during, 14, 124; reasons
for ending, 20, 132, 144n10, 145n18;
purpose of, 21, 22, 77, 131, 141n2,
145n2, 151n12
—on itinerancy: contribution to
knowledge on, 2–3, 135–40 passim;
doctoral thesis, 3, 14, 132; later work
for California Immigration
Commission, 20, 312; distinctive
itinerant groups, 21, 78, 95, 100–
101; hardships of itinerant life, 28,
35–36, 37–39, 49, 101, 121, 125,
128, 130, 136–37, 151n10; dual
labor markers, 63, 74
—on IWW, 116; on itinerants'
comments about, 117–19; divergent
appeal of, 119–20; on acceptance
among itinerants, 120–121, 127–28;
conversation with recruiter, 122–23;

on visits to locals, 124–27; battle of
hymns incident, 129–30
—on lumber industry: Hume camp, 41,
42, 43, 55–56; Hume flume, 42, 43,
85–86; Millwood, 43–44; workers,
43, 45, 47, 52, 58–59, 59–60; nature
of work, 45, 47–48, 48–49, 57–58,
59, 60–61, 62–63; on Tony, 49, 50–
51, 53; on Russian hobo, 49–50;
camp life, 54–56; comparison of
lumber and orange workers, 55, 63;
report recommendations, 64
—on orange industry, 14, 22–26, 28,
29–30, 31–39; working conditions,
25, 26, 28, 37; effects of packing, 29,
37–39; summary of industry
conditions, 39
—on railroads: ways to ride trains, 96,
97, 100–14 passim; first experience
riding trains, 96–97, 99–101;
itinerants' conversations, 101–4; trip
from Chico to Sacramento, 105–7;
conversations with shacks, 107, 108,
110, 111; on last trip, 108–12; on
itinerants' stories, 112–13; on
decking train in full view, 113–14
—on road construction, 65–66, 68, 72–
75; in novel, 68–72. See also
Employment agency game
—on the road, 82–87; poem, 76–77; on
jungles, 78–80; on itinerants, 81–82,
88–90, 90–95, 150n4
Mills, Robert (son of Frederick C.), 15
Mills, William H. (son of Frederick C.),
ix, xi
Millwood. See Hume-Bennett Lumber
Company
Minkler, California, 87, 117; Mills in,
85, 86

National Bureau of Economic Research:
and Mills, 16, 17
"New Immigration": attitude toward
bosses, 30

Oakland, California, 135; and Kelley's
Army, 9; Mills in, 12, 14; and
railroads, 101
Olsen, Jake, 56
One-spot (train): at Hume, 44–45, 51–
52

Orange industry: history around Lindsay, 22, 23; impact on employees, 37–39; workers compared to lumber workers, 55, 63; workers and the IWW, 119, 120; after Mills's trip, 134. *See also* Drake orange packinghouse; Mills, Frederick C.

Oregon Express (train), 111

Otis, Marcus (IWW speaker): and Mills, 125, 126

Pacific Northwest: and itinerant workers, 78

Panama Canal, 10, 80

Parker, Carleton H., 11; on itinerant labor, 11, 12, 57, 132; on IWW, 11, 122; and California Immigration Commission, 11–12, 132–33; and Mills's trip, 12, 14, 132; on number of California itinerants, 20, 21, 39, 63; CIR testimony, 20, 132; on Wheatland riot, 24; report on California employment agencies, 66–68; IWW attitude toward, 126, 152n13

Parker, Cornelia Stratton: on Mills's catching malaria, 132, 144n10

Pleasant Grove, California: and railroads, 107

Portland, Oregon: and railroads, 110; and the IWW, 118

Railroads. *See* Mills, Frederick C.; Railroad shacks and bulls; United States Interstate Commerce Commission

Railroad shacks and bulls: interactions of, with itinerants, 96, 97, 100–14 passim; allowing itinerants to ride, 107–8, 109–10, 123; taking money from itinerants, 110, 113

Red Bluff, California: and railroads, 109, 110, 111, 113

Redding, California, 119, 129; as northern end of Mills's trip, 1, 20; and railroads, 108, 110, 111, 112; and the IWW, 126–27

Reedley, California, 41, 65, 69, 86; Mills in, 85

Road construction: in California, 65; after Mills's trip, 134. *See also* Ball (road contractor); Employment agency game; Mills, Frederick C.

Rogers, Professor (character in Mills's novel), 135–40

Roseville, California: and railroads, 104, 106, 113

Russian hobo (at Hume). *See* Mills, Frederick C.: on lumber industry

Sacramento, California, 20, 82, 105, 113, 117, 118, 121; and Kelley's Army, 9; employment agencies in, 67, 104; and railroads, 101, 104, 106, 107, 108, 112; and the IWW, 104, 122, 123, 124–26, 129–30

Sacramento Valley, California: and Mills's trip, 17, 20

Sand Creek Road, 65–73 passim, 82, 99. *See also* Ball (road contractor); Mills, Frederick C.: on road construction

San Diego, California: and IWW free speech fight, 116

San Francisco, California, 14, 91, 140; and Kelley's Army, 9; unemployment in, 9, 137, 138; Immigration Commission report on tenements in, 12; as Immigration Commission headquarters, 20, 22, 108, 131; and Industrial Relations Committee hearings, 20, 133, 137; employment agencies in, 67; and the IWW, 122; and Commonwealth Club, 137, 140

Sanger, California, 41, 49, 52; and Hume-Bennett Lumber Company, 42; Mills in, 85; itinerants in jungle, 90–92; itinerants at railroad station, 93–95

San Joaquin Valley, California, 82; and Mills's trip, 17, 20, 21

Santa Fe Railroad, 85, 87

Scott (IWW speaker), 126

Seasonal workers. *See* Itinerant workers

Selma, California, 99, 117; and railroads, 101

Sierra Nevada Mountains, 17, 23, 39, 41, 44, 69

Sinclair, Upton, 128

Smith-Moore Lumber Company. *See* Hume-Bennett Lumber Company

Social Science Research Council: and Mills, 16
Sonoma County, California: Immigration Commission report on, 12
Speek, Peter A.: on the IWW, 122; and the Industrial Relations Commission, 122
Stockton California, 96, 112, 126; and railroads, 99, 101; itinerant begging in, 103; and asylum inmate story, 103; and the IWW, 108, 115, 122
Suhr, Herman D., 124, 128; IWW leader at Wheatland, 6; itinerants' comments on, 117, 118, 123, 126
Sydenstricker, Edgar: on pre–World War I itinerancy, 2; on California seasonal work, 20
Syndicalism: and the IWW, 115

Tony (Italian lumbercamp worker). See Mills, Frederick C.: on lumber industry
Tramps. See Itinerant workers
Tulare, California, 41, 82, 85; Mills in, 83; marshal cursed by itinerant, 89
Tulare County, California, 31; and job ads for orange workers, 22–24; history of agriculture in, 23; and Sand Creek Road project, 65, 66, 68, 72; sheriff praised, 89

Unemployment: studies on pre–World War I, 2–3; among itinerant workers, 9, 137, 138; and public employment agencies, 72–74, 149n8
University of California, Berkeley. See Mills, Frederick C.: background
United States Commission on Industrial Relations (CIR), 135; overview of work, 10; and Carleton Parker, 20, 132; San Francisco hearings, 20, 132, 133, 137; reports, 24, 66–68; on public employment agencies, 72, 73; and Peter Speek, 122; policy recommendations, 133–34, 137
United States Department of Justice: and the IWW, 134

United States Interstate Commerce Commission: on illegal train riders killed, 97

Visalia, California, 41, 69, 83, 85; Mills in, 84

Washington, D.C.: and Kelley's Army, 9, 138
Weed, California: and railroads, 109
Western (train): and Mills, 105, 106, 113
Wheatland, California, 5, 125; planned demonstration in, 117, 121, 124, 126, 127, 128, 151n12. See also Wheatland riot
Wheatland riot, 22, 131; account of events, 5–6; and the IWW, 5–6, 116, 150n3; as incentive to investigate itinerancy, 9, 10; and Immigration Commission, 11, 12; role of job ads in, 24
Wobblies. See Industrial Workers of the World
World War I, ix, 9, 10, 64; and itinerants, 78; and the IWW, 115, 134; effect of, on itinerant issues, 131; Immigration Commission activities during, 133; and the Industrial Relations Commission, 133
Workers: American, 26, 30, 57, 66, 69, 89, 91, 95; American Indian, 6, 87; Armenian, 6, 65; Asian, 30; Asian Indian, 6, 65, 69, 70; Austrian, 111; black, 92; Chinese, 6; English, 81; Filipino, 6; German, 57, 58; Greek, 47, 52, 57, 58, 79; Irish, 47, 57, 101, 102, 103, 124; Italian, 44, 47, 49, 50–51, 52, 57, 58, 79; Japanese, 6, 86, 89, 91, 95, 117; Mexican, 6, 52, 65, 69, 86, 91, 95; New England, 57, 77; Puerto Rican, 118; Russian, 44, 49–50, 57, 58, 63; Scottish, 57, 94; Slavic, 69, 101–2; Southern European, 12, 26, 79; Swedish, 48, 56, 57, 58. See also Itinerant workers
Wyckoff, Walter: on hobo life, 1; compared to Mills, 77

Note on the Author

Gregory R. Woirol is Professor of Economics at Whittier College in California. He received his Ph.D. in economics from the University of California, Berkeley, in 1980. His articles have been published in such journals as *Labor History, California History,* and *Southern California Quarterly.*

DATE DUE

DIS FEB 21 1994

BRODART, INC.

Cat. No. 23-221